Developing a Heavenly Mind Control

Devotional Thoughts to Reboot
Our Minds with Truth

Linda Killian

Copyright © 2015 Linda Killian

Cover photo: Creative Travel Projects, via Shutterstock.com

Author photo: David Studarus

Publishing services provided by PEP Writing Services through BrendaStrohbehn.com

All rights reserved. No portion of this material may be reproduced or distributed without the written permission of Linda Killian and/or her legal representative(s). Brief portions may be quoted for review purposes.

ESV: Portions taken from the English Standard Version are marked with (ESV) following the Scripture reference.

Holman Christian Standard Bible®
Copyright © 1999, 2000, 2002, 2003, 2009 by Holman Bible Publishers.
Used with permission by Holman Bible Publishers, Nashville, Tennessee.
All rights reserved.

Portions quoted from the King James Version are in the public domain.

Scripture taken from The Message. Copyright © 1993, 1994, 1995, 1996, 2000, 2001, 2002. Used by permission of NavPress Publishing Group.

NASB: Scripture taken from the NEW AMERICAN STANDARD BIBLE®, Copyright © 1960, 1962, 1963, 1968, 1971, 1972, 1973, 1975, 1977, 1995 by The Lockman Foundation. Used by permission.

Scripture taken from the New King James Version®. Copyright © 1982 by Thomas Nelson. Used by permission. All rights reserved.

Unless otherwise noted, all Scripture is quoted from the New International Version
NIV: THE HOLY BIBLE, NEW INTERNATIONAL VERSION®, NIV®
Copyright © 1973, 1978, 1984, 2011 by Biblica, Inc.® Used by permission.
All rights reserved worldwide.

NLT: Scripture quotations marked (NLT) are taken from the Holy Bible, New Living Translation, copyright © 1996, 2004, 2007 by Tyndale House Foundation. Used by permission of Tyndale House Publishers, Inc., Carol Stream, Illinois 60188.

ISBN: 1517467101
ISBN-13: 978-1517467104

To my mom, Rose Marie Van Loh, who wanted a new devotional book to read each morning; thank you for your earnest prayers for me every morning in the middle bedroom (following my high school years) and for continuing to pray for my family and me yet today

CONTENTS

Introduction 1

Duct Tape to the Rescue 5

Makeup Mirror 9

Loneliness 13

Will This Matter or Count for Eternity? 17

Wisdom 21

Hope 25

Disappointment 29

Shema 33

Foolishness 37

Mind Control 41

Never Be Shaken 45

Safety Net 49

Trust Me 53

Snare and Deadfall Traps 57

What's Next, Papa? 61

Duracell vs. Energizer® 65

The Three Rs 69

Off Balance 73

Be Quick and Be Slow 77

What I Don't Know and Do Know 81

Temporary Residence 85

Just Obedience 89

Diligently Staying on Course 93

A. S. K.	97
Buckle Up!	101
Never on Hold	105
Inevitable	109
Living the Life	113
A Free Gift—490 Times	117
Giving a Blessing	121
Give Me Joy!	125
Aphids	129
Waiting Expectantly	133
Self-Control	137
When I Grow Up	143
Enslaved by Uncertainty	149
Harvest Time	153
The Helper	157
Tomorrow	161
I Have Everything I Need	165
About the Author	169

INTRODUCTION

Colossians 3:2 states, "Set your minds on things that are above, not on things that are on the earth." I have a passion for God's Word, and I want to share several devotional thoughts to help us "set our minds above" at the beginning of each new day.

My mother, whose name is Rose (both my granddaughter Harper and I have the middle name "Rose" in honor of my mother), shared with me that she wanted a new devotional book to read. She said she had read through the Bible each year, but that while doing so, it made her feel pressured to just get it done. Though she received blessings every year in doing it, now, in her later years, she wished for something shorter to start her day out with: a rich nugget from God's Word that would speak to her as she began her day.

I decided to personally provide that desire for my mother in the form of this devotional book that she can read and meditate on. I also wanted to honor her by having my second published book in her hands, giving her Scripture verses and biblical thoughts with which to start her day. My purpose in this book is to have devotional thoughts not too long in length but that are quick and helpful in drawing our minds toward thoughts of heavenly things before the day-to-day earthly tasks. I also hope that you will have a, "Me too! I can totally relate!" experience as you grow in your daily walk and in your relationship with the Lord. Some of these devotionals come from deep inside my heart from various firsthand trials and lessons I have learned. May they glorify God and uplift your heart.

Satan's weapons of temptations to us are guilt, shame, frustration, and failure. These thoughts can play havoc with your life as they do with mine. Think about it: What causes you to have feelings of defeat? When do you totally feel defeated? Is it because of thoughts of guilt? Is it because of thoughts of total shame and embarrassment? Are you totally frustrated? Do you feel like a failure over a situation and then feel all alone? There you go! Satan's subtle attacks within our thoughts must be redirected to right thinking. I remember that Zig Ziglar called it "stinkin' thinkin'!"

I personally struggle with this frequently, since I am a people pleaser and tend to be a perfectionist. Therefore, I am declaring war against false thoughts and arming myself with truth. I want to have a manual for "right thinking." I want to have my sword of God's Word ready for the next battle the enemy throws at me. I want to replace false thoughts with truths from God's Word and have a mind that is set on heavenly things, which are above. As Paul admonished the church in Philippi, in Philippians 4:8: "Finally, brothers, whatever is true, whatever is honorable, whatever is just, whatever is pure, whatever is lovely, whatever is commendable, if there is *any* excellence, if there is *anything* worthy of praise, think about *these* things" (emphasis mine). Paul chose thirty-six words for that long sentence. Let's explore replacing wrong thoughts with truth from God's Word in this devotional book so that we can, "In all circumstances take up the shield of faith, with which you can extinguish all the flaming darts of the evil one..." (Ephesians 6:16).

We need to arm ourselves daily. The purpose of this book is to provide a thought for the day with which you can arm yourself with God's shield of protection to defeat the roaring lion who is waiting to pounce and rear up his loud roar against you. You will tame the lion's roar by thinking truthful thoughts. You will develop a godly mind control with Scripture that moves eighteen inches in length—the measurement between your head and your heart. Ephesians 6:13 states: "Therefore take up the whole armor of God, that you may be able to withstand in the evil day, and having done all to *stand firm*" (emphasis mine).

At the end of each devotional you will find the name of a corresponding song from a Christian artist. I would like to encourage you to watch and listen to that, perhaps on YouTube. God has often ministered to me through special songs in my life. My desire is that the songs I have chosen will help impress into your memory the promises of God in arming your mind in God's shield of truth from His Word.

You will also find a statement at the end of each devotional that says, "My prayer requests for today are." I believe that we need more prayer warriors. Again, let me encourage you to write down your prayer requests and needs at the end of each devotional. Let this be a place where you can write them out, pray for them, and review them often.

May God give you a new thought and direction for each day as you use this devotional book to help keep your mind on heavenly things and to see and experience the light of God's truths. May your mind be rebooted with God's Word so that you can "set your minds on things that are above, not on things that are on earth" (Colossians 3:2).

DUCT TAPE TO THE RESCUE

Isaiah 40:28–29, 31: "The LORD is everlasting God, the Creator of the ends of the earth. He does not faint or grow weary; His understanding is unsearchable. He gives power to the faint, and to him who has no might He increases strength…but they who wait for the LORD shall renew their strength; they shall mount up with wings like eagles; they shall run and not be weary; they shall walk and not faint."

Have you ever noticed that when you're exhausted, things come out of your mouth wrong and often harshly? Your intentions are misunderstood. Instances forgotten come flaring back up in your mind. Hurtful words you received in the past somehow return to your thoughts again. When this happens, do you say things that you later wish you could take back? I do! You yearn for your words to be in playback and edit mode! While under duress from being worn out, I have written things that got misinterpreted or received entirely differently from my purpose.

Patience becomes a stranger when I am tired. Things get all twisted and out of proportion when my nerves are raw, and my emotions are exposed when my energy is gone. Instead of holding my tongue I find myself later regretting what came out. At least that is how it is with me, particularly when I have had a lack of sleep.

Recently, my husband and I were both totally exhausted from working on a project together. The other people involved in this project were all pulling their own weight and working very hard to get this project completed within a narrow time frame. Each of us was totally worn out physically and emotionally, and yet we knew beyond a shadow of doubt that this project was completely orchestrated by God. Yet it seemed that the days were not long enough. Two to four hours of sleep at night were the norm for several weeks.

My husband said to me, "Don't think old. Don't think tired. Think energetic!" However he would get very short with me and I with him during this particular episode in our life. It's amazing how exhaustion can cause misunderstandings. In times like that, our patience is tested—just as Satan tried to tempt the Lord in Matthew 4:1–11, but that is another story and study in itself!

Perhaps I should have worn duct tape over my mouth (which might not have been a bad idea) when my body was exhausted and my emotions were raw. Yet I am so thankful that the LORD "does not faint or grow weary; His understanding is unsearchable. He gives *power* to the faint, and to him who has *no might* He increases strength…" (Isaiah 40:28–29, 31). When I read this, I can picture an eagle with outspread wings, soaring high in the sky and sailing over our valley.

Eagles are strong birds, known and admired for symbolizing power. Eagles' eyes have a million light-sensitive cells per square millimeter of retina, which is five times more than that of humans' two hundred thousand cells. Because of this, eagles have extremely keen eyesight. Their vision is the sharpest of any animal. They can spot an animal the size of a rabbit two miles away. Just as an eagle spreads its wings to signify its massive strength, God spreads His wings over us in His power, His strength, and His protection of us. His vision goes far beyond what we can see, so sometimes we need to wait and trust in the LORD, because he knows any distress we may be in. Strength is available to us when we draw close to God, so we can "run and not be weary...."

"Lord, fill me with all of Your fullness. Give me strength. You are able to do more abundantly than all I ask or think, according to Your power at work within me, as Ephesians 3:14–21 declares."

Now I will *take off* the duct tape and *put on* God's strength to carry me through my day on His wings of power, vitality, courage, durability, and tenacity!

Psalm 119:28 states: "My soul melts away for sorrow, strengthen me according to your word!"

Listen to: "It's One of Those Days, Lord," by Joseph Cheetham-Wilkenson.

My thoughts and prayer requests for today are:

MAKEUP MIRROR

I have a magnifying makeup mirror in my bathroom that I use every morning. I have a separate makeup mirror that I use to check the back of my hair after I blow dry it. This one is smaller in size, and I can take it with me when I travel and stay overnight somewhere. I am lost without my magnifying mirrors: without a magnifying mirror, I can't get my eyeliner on correctly anymore. And I have to use the portable mirror to make sure all of the hairs are in place. It all needs to be smooth and in place.

The Bible is God's mirror to help us check what we have in place and what we don't have in place in our walk with Christ. James 1:23–25 tells us, "For if anyone is a hearer of the word and not a doer, he is like a man who looks intently at his natural face in a mirror. For he looks at himself and goes away and at once forgets what he was like. But the one who looks into the perfect law, the law of liberty, and perseveres, being no hearer who forgets but a doer who acts, he will be blessed in his doing."

Just as I check my physical appearance in my mirrors, so I must check the spiritual condition of my heart and mind in God's Word continually. God's Word is the spiritual mirror of my very soul. I need to examine myself every day and check my thinking with God's Word. I must ask myself if my feelings are coinciding with truths from God's Word. I must see if I am having "right thinking" by dwelling on: "whatever is honorable, whatever is just, whatever is pure, whatever is lovely, whatever is commendable," as it says in Philippians 4:8.

I must deal with my spiritual appearance before Christ and confess any sin that might have crept in. As Colossians 2:6 states: "Therefore, as you received Christ Jesus the Lord, so walk in him." This means that I must evaluate how I walk my life with Christ every day: Am I reflecting Christ's image before others? Am I mirroring Christ? Am I surrendering my will to Christ as my Lord, Savior, and Master?

My two magnifying mirrors don't lie. They show me any hairs not in place. They show me if I have any of those spots from my mascara on my eyelids over my eyeshadow. (How I hate that!)

God's Word is our spiritual mirror to examine our spiritual appearance. We need to check any part of our lives that are not rightly in place with Him, and we must persevere, as it says in James 1:23–25 in the NLT: "For if you listen to the word, and don't obey, it is like glancing at your face in the mirror. You see yourself, walk away, and forget what you look like. But if you look into the perfect law that sets you free, and if you do what it says and don't forget what you heard, then God will bless you for doing it."

Listen to: "To You Oh Lord I Lift up My Soul (Psalm 25)," by Graham Kendrick.

My thoughts and prayer requests for today are:

LONELINESS

Deuteronomy 31:6, 8: "Be strong and courageous. Do not fear or be in dread of them, for it is the Lord your God who goes with you. He will not leave you or forsake you. And the LORD, He is the one who goes before you. He will be with you. He will not leave you nor forsake you, do not fear nor be dismayed."

Do you ever feel lonely? Do you ever feel isolated? Do you ever feel that people just don't understand you? I sometimes do. When going through a major trial, have you hit a few days where you have felt all alone? I've had that too. Do you ever wonder if others are praying for you as much as you are praying for them?

I sometimes have these thoughts. I have felt totally alone, and yet I have known that friends were praying, and I have known that God was with me. But I just felt all alone.

This is another battle to fight in order to have a new and heavenly mind control—one where the old was replaced with the truths from God's Word. The Lord walks right beside us. He follows us. He goes before us. He will never leave us. Nothing will happen to us that He has not first allowed for the benefit of our lives. I don't want any woman to feel she is all alone while undergoing any trial, because I have sometimes felt like that in the past too, and it simply is false.

When the enemy tempts you with feelings that you are just not good enough and you are a failure, loneliness creeps in. Instead, replace those thoughts with the assurance that God loves you. He goes before you. He will be with you. He will not leave you or turn His back on you. He works everything out in your life for His good purposes. Instead of looking inward, look upward and outward. Seek to be a friend to someone. Pray and ask God, "Who can I encourage today? Who needs a friend? I will be that friend!"

As Proverbs 11:25 says, "Whoever brings blessing will be enriched, and one who waters will himself be watered." Seek to be a blessing to some other woman. Ask God to put in your mind a woman who needs an encouraging word from you today. Remember the trial you went through? (You may be thinking, "Which one—there have been so many?") There is some needy woman that is waiting for the perfect encouragement that only you can give! Who do you need to be praying for? When you walk into church, look for a woman you can make eye contact with and give her a big smile. Extend an invitation to a woman to go to coffee or tea with you—or even lunch. Increase your hospitality skills. But you may wonder what you should make and serve in regards to food: everyone likes grilled cheese sandwiches. Top it off with girl talk. It doesn't have to be fancy to fill a need.

Be strong and courageous. Reach out and be a friend to someone in need today. Ask the Holy Spirit to lay someone in need of a friend on your heart. You'll see the blessings that result from being a blessing to another woman. There may be a risk in showing vulnerability, but you may never know that woman is in a crisis similar to one you've known unless you open up and are willing to share. Loneliness will then fade away and be replaced with the joy of being a blessing to someone else in need of a friend. Proverbs 11:24 (NKJV) says, "A man who has friends must himself be friendly. But there is a friend that sticks closer than a brother."

Remember, you are not alone. God is right beside you. Lean close to Him. He is waiting to listen to your need. He has preapproved you. He will protect you. He will be your shield. Reach out to a woman in need and be the friend a sister in the Lord needs, and the blessing will be returned to you! Go and walk in the presence of Christ.

Listen to: "I Am Not Alone," by Kari Jobe.

My thoughts and prayer requests for today are:

_____

_____

_____

_____

_____

_____

_____

_____

_____

_____

_____

_____

_____

_____

_____

_____

_____

WILL THIS MATTER OR COUNT FOR ETERNITY?

Colossians 3:1–2: "If then you have been raised with Christ, seek the things that are above, where Christ is, seated at the right hand of God. Set your minds on things that are above, not on things that are on the earth."

I was teaching on Colossians 3:1–4 in our Women of the Word ministry at my church. The title I had been given to teach on was "Mind Control." I had three points:

1. There is victory in seeking a mind-set focused on the realities of heaven.
2. There is victory in our mind being focused on: So, will this matter or count in eternity?
3. There is victory in Jesus. Eternity is our reward and we will share in God's glory.

I had been praying for God to give me just the right illustrations for my teaching of just these four verses in this passage. I studied. I practiced in front of the island in my kitchen as I watched the timer on my stove count down the forty minutes of time to teach as I rehearsed my lesson time and time again.

I got to church for the morning session, arriving in plenty of time to collect myself and make sure that everything was set up correctly—or so I thought. However, much to my horror, when looking at the monitor, all of the slides from our Colossians session were gone! They were simply gone. The only slides that were there were from previous video Bible studies. I was in a panic since there were two slides that I needed to have on the large screens as I taught.

In my mind, computers are supposed to work—period. Thank goodness our media director came in and rescued my problem! He showed me that someone had inadvertently deleted them. He simply typed in "Colossians" at a spot that said "Library," and…voilà! Everything returned!

The next problem arose when the mic that I had over my ear stopped working when I was up on the platform and started to speak. Not a problem: someone brought me the handheld mic. Later that afternoon, right before I left for church to teach the evening session, I had to hunt for my cell phone for fifteen minutes! When I arrived at church that evening, the spotlights were blinding me when I was setting up the room. I tried every switch and button on the light console, and nothing changed. We found the solution to that, and thankfully, I wasn't blinded by the lights aiming for my left eye anymore. Okay, I could breathe and stop feeling frenzied.

As I was rereading my lesson in a private room before going up to teach that evening, it was as if the Holy Spirit tapped me on the shoulder and said, "Linda, you need to know something! You are going to laugh at yourself! I gave you several illustrations today for your point on: 'Okay, so will this count or matter for eternity?' You missed it! Remember the Colossian's slides, the mic, hunting for your cell phone, and the blinding spotlights? Remember the stress you allowed yourself to feel over things not going just right as you thought they should? There you go! You have another vivid and fresh illustration for Colossians 3:1–4, regarding your lesson on having a spiritual mind controlled by Christ. Now go share it with the women tonight!"

What a spectacular future awaits us! We must not fix our minds on the temporary things in life. We need to spend more time on thinking about precious promises of insight, knowledge, and wisdom from God's Word rather than dwelling on what we are going to wear or what recipe to make. We need to spend more time in His presence, to be quiet, and to sit before Him.

This world is not our home (there is an old song by that very title), and we have a future with Christ, who is seated at the right hand of God. Look at life through heaven's point of view. Breathe in salvation. Breathe out hope. Strive to live in the presence of Christ and have that be your heavenly mind-set. Colossians 3:2 is the goal for today: "Lord, set my 'mind on things that are above, not on things that are on the earth.'"

Listen to: "This Is the Stuff," by Francesca Battistelli.

My thoughts and prayer requests for today are:

WISDOM

Proverbs 2:6–7: "For the LORD gives wisdom; from his mouth come knowledge and understanding; he stores up sound wisdom for the upright; he is a shield to those who walk in integrity."

James 1:5: "If any of you lacks wisdom, let him ask God, who gives generously to all without reproach, and it will be given him."

Do you ever need guidance in making a decision? There are times when we don't want to make a mistake, and we want to make the right choice. Or do you ever feel you need to be smarter and not be lacking in intelligence? I do. So often I have asked the Lord, "Oh please, help me not to say stupid stuff today!"

Proverbs 2:6–7 tells us: "The LORD gives wisdom." And Job 32:8 explains: "But it is the spirit in man, the breath of the Almighty, that makes him understand."

Warren Wiersbe said that knowledge is the ability to take things apart, while wisdom is the ability to put them together. It has also been said that a person doesn't learn from his successes but his mistakes. Growing in character comes from learning from mistakes. God has promised to give us wisdom, and Proverbs 2:6–7 tells us that He "gives wisdom." God even "stores up sound wisdom" as you walk in His presence. He is your shield as you walk in righteousness and integrity.

Two simple words: "He gives." He gives what? "Wisdom."

James 1:5 is the promise to cling to when you ask God for wisdom. It states that He will give it to you "generously." God is not stingy. If you ask Him for wisdom, He will give it to you abundantly, lavishly, amply, bountifully, liberally, and openhandedly. So ask God to help you understand and to use the circumstances you are in for His glory. Ask and you shall receive (Matthew 7:7).

Listen to: "Sacred Place," by Gwen Smith.

My thoughts and prayer requests for today are:

HOPE

Romans 15:13 states: "May the God of hope fill you with all joy and peace in believing, so that by the power of the Holy Spirit you may abound in hope."

Distractions in life diminish our hope and deplete our joy and peace. But David said in Psalm 119:50, "This is my comfort in my affliction, that your promise gives me life." Joy and peace come from trusting in God.

Our various hopes play out in our mind whether we are conscious of them or not. We will still pray that what we hope will happen, will happen. Yet how often we fret and worry until a situation is resolved.

"An expectation of fulfillment" is one way to define the word *hope*. Another definition is: "a strong desire." However, God expects us to have a confident expectation, an expectation of fulfillment, and a strong desire in knowing that our prayers will be answered according to His will, as it says in Romans 8:28: "And we know that for those that love God all things work together for good…."

Know God. Have confidence that God is working behind the scenes in ways you don't even know about. Remember God's protection and help for you as stated in Jeremiah 29:11: "For I know the plans I have for you, declares the LORD, plans to prosper you and not to harm you, plans to give you hope and a future."

Dwell on the word *hope* today and ask God to show you knew and mighty things you have not seen before about Him. Replace thoughts of despair with hope in God's power.

"May the God of hope fill you with all joy and peace in believing, so that by the power of the Holy Spirit you may abound in hope" (Romans 15:13). My word for today is *hope*, and I will replace my hopelessness with joy and peace by believing that God has this!

Listen to: "Take Heart," by Hillsong United.

My thoughts and prayer requests for today are:

DISAPPOINTMENT

Romans 5:5, NLT: "And this hope will not leave us to disappointment. For we know how dearly God loves us, because He has given us the Holy Spirit to fill our hearts with His love."

Disappointment is a feeling of sadness or displeasure because something was not as good as expected or because something you hoped for or expected did not happen. Sadness, regret, dismay, defeat, and sorrow are of the emotions that come into play when dealing with disappointments. We rehearse or daydream in our mind our expectations about a trip or an event, and when it does not go as we expected it to, we might feel let down or feel utterly defeated. Or maybe a relationship with someone let you down. There are even certain words that can cut and hurt deeply, and when they do, thoughts of disappointment come rushing in.

It is all about our expectations. Satan plays on these times. He knows that when we are discouraged he can steal our joy in our walk with Christ, and then we will not be the person God intends for us to be. I have fallen into this trap time and time again. I have noticed that when I dwell on my disappointment in a situation, it can take me two or even three days to retrain my mind to think instead about things above (Colossians 3:1–4). Instead, I need to think about God working everything out for my good (Romans 8:28) and remember that God is my shield and protector (Genesis 15:1 and Psalm 28:7).

Disappointment often leads us into thinking about just giving up. I can think of a situation in my life in which I often think, "I am not going to get hurt anymore by this! I have had enough. That's it! I am done!" However, I must replace those thoughts by thinking about endurance, patience, joy, peace, longsuffering, love, and how God is molding me into His image—even through disappointments. I must have endurance, try to curb my expectations, and not dwell on *me*.

Do you realize that when we are not thankful, it is like we are telling God that He has not done a good enough job in our life? Doesn't He promise to work out everything for our good and form us into His image? Think about that for a few minutes. Have you ever felt hurt when you tried your best to do something nice for someone and it didn't turn out quite right? You tried to do it perfectly, but something about it was less than perfect, or the recipient did not receive it in the way you had intended? Were you hurt or even disappointed that he or she didn't show thankfulness for your efforts?

There go those expectations again.

Prayer is a powerful weapon in fighting disappointments and discouragement. Pour out your heart to God. Ask Him what He wants you to learn from the situations that did not live up to your expectations. When I am on my way back up from working through a disappointment in life, I often sing the song, "This world is not my home, I'm just a passing through. My treasures are laid up somewhere beyond the blue."

My Grandma Helmers would often tell me as a child, "This too shall pass." What she meant by that was God knows the end of whatever we are going through. God is sovereign. God is in control of our days. "We are either going through a trial or just coming out of one," as my pastor, Todd Smith, often states.

Once we experience victory over our disappointment, we can then have victory in Christ in our mind control, replacing the dismay and defeat of our disappointment with true peace and joy that only come from being filled with the Holy Spirit.

Ask yourself again," Okay, will this count or matter for eternity?"

Our hope in God, "will not leave us to disappointment. For we know how dearly God loves us, because He has given us the Holy Spirit to fill our hearts with His love" (Romans 5:5).

Battling a disappointment? Pray for God to replace your disappointment by filling your heart with love, joy, hope, and peace as He sustains you in your walk with Him. You may just have to do this over and over and over again until you have victory in fully transferring it over to God. Replace thoughts of disappointment with hope and thankfulness. Start thinking about all of the things you are thankful for instead of all of the things you are disappointed about. Have a thankful heart. Dwell on thankfulness rather than on disappointment.

Listen to: "Broken into Beautiful," by Gwen Smith.

My thoughts and prayer requests for today are:

SHEMA

Matthew 22:37–38: "You shall love the Lord your God with all your heart and with all your soul and with all your mind. This is the great and first commandment."

In Mark 12:30, Jesus is also recorded as saying: "And you shall love the Lord your God with all your heart and with all your soul and with all your mind and with all your strength."

Matthew wrote that we are to love the Lord with all of our heart, soul, and mind. But Mark wrote that we are to love the Lord with all of our heart, soul, mind, and strength.

Now again in Luke 10:27, Luke is writing about the parable of the Good Samaritan and states what was written in the law: "You shall love the Lord your God with all your heart and with all your soul and with all your strength and with all your mind, and your neighbor as yourself."

Jesus quoted the Shema, which is the Jewish prayer book. It was the source of what was often the first verse a Jewish child learned: Deuteronomy 6:4, which is where these three verses from Matthew, Mark, and Luke had their origin. It was a statement of faith that was recited daily by orthodox Jews, both morning and evening (the word *Shema* comes from the Hebrew word that means "to hear"). "Hear, O Israel: The Lord your God, the Lord is one." Then in Deuteronomy 6:5, Moses, when he summoned the Israelites regarding the Ten Commandments, said, "You shall love the Lord your God with all your heart and with all your soul and with all your might." This was the first and greatest commandment from God.

Service and obedience will result from loving the Lord our God with all of our heart, soul, mind, strength, and might. That makes up our whole being. That about says it all. When I am seeking to love my God with all of my heart, soul, mind, strength, and yes, might, there is no room left for not loving others. It is already consumed with the things of God. We must be consumed and preoccupied with thinking on heavenly things and seeking the things that are above (Colossians 3:1–4) instead of the mundane things on this earth. It takes persistence. It takes diligence. It takes humility. Being in the Word of God daily, being eager to pray and honor God in all things, and continually having a mind-set that dwells on all Christ has done for us must be the priority. Our love for Him will then grow and flourish, and then it will spill out into having love for others.

"But, they hurt me when they said that! Or, "But they hurt me when they treated me that way!" No, unloving attitudes have to be replaced with love, grace, and mercy toward the unlovely people in our lives. Let God settle the score. He has a bigger hammer than we do. There really are no more excuses.

Listen to: "Word of God Speak," by MercyMe."

My thoughts and prayer requests for today are:

FOOLISHNESS

Romans 12:16 (NKJV): "Be of the same mind toward one another. Do not set your mind on high things, but associate with the humble. Do not be wise in your own opinion."

    The HCSB states: "Do not be wise in your own estimation."

    The ESV states: "Never be wise in your own sight."

The NLT states it yet another way: "Live in harmony with each other. Don't be too proud to enjoy the company of ordinary people. And don't think you know it all."

God's gift of grace to us is exemplified in Romans 12:3 (ESV), which also says: "For by the grace given to me I say to everyone among you not to think of himself more highly than he ought to think, but to think with sober judgment, each according to the measure of faith that God has assigned."

Isn't it easy to see a lack of humility in other people? But I have had to look inward and ask: Do I think I am wise, because it is my opinion? Do I make an immediate outward estimation of others? Do I talk or give the impression that I think I know it all, and that my opinion is superior? I shudder to think that I have done that too many times. I realize that apart from God I am hopeless and helpless, and my opinion may not really matter. What counts for eternity is what really matters.

When a person is humble he or she has wisdom. They go hand in hand. Proverbs 19:20 states: "Listen to advice and accept instruction, that you may gain wisdom in the future. Proverbs 22:4 states: "The reward for humility and fear of the Lord is riches and honor and life."

We are told in Proverbs 28:26: "Whoever trusts in his own mind is a fool, be he who walks in wisdom will be delivered." Then there is my favorite verse of all in regards to a "fool," and that is found in Proverbs 17:28: "Even a fool who keeps silent is considered wise; when he closes his lips, he is deemed intelligent." Wow. If I were to simply keep my mouth shut I may have the opportunity to demonstrate wisdom as I show grace and mercy to others. I will actually then be the wiser person, showing greater wisdom from the life God has given me so far.

Romans 12:3 tells me to: "think with sober judgment." When someone is thinking, he or she is not necessarily speaking. Sometimes it is better not to have to take our foot out of our mouth or need duct tape but, instead, to walk in wisdom, humbly, not having to be delivered from embarrassment.

Listen to: "Listen," by Josh Wilson.

My thoughts and prayer requests for today are:

MIND CONTROL

Romans 12:2: "Do not be conformed to this world, but be transformed by the renewal of your mind, that by testing you may discern what is the will of God, what is good and acceptable and perfect.:

What controls your mind? Does today's list of appointments, groceries, commitments, and responsibilities control your thoughts? Where does your mind go when you get just a few seconds to daydream? Are your thoughts about a verse that spoke to you recently or a worship song that you recently listened to? God wants to be first in your thoughts. God wants to control your mind through His Word. God wants to replace your first thought about what you have to get done today with His Word. God wants to transform you "by the renewal of your mind," helping you to learn and gain more knowledge of God, as it says in Colossians 3:10 "...the new self, which is being renewed in knowledge after the image of its creator."

The word *transform* describes having a change from within. Warren Wiersbe says: "The world wants to change your mind, so it exerts pressure from without. But the Holy Spirit changes your mind by releasing power from within." Do you conform to today's cultural way of thinking, or do you have a mind-set that is actively being transformed by studying and reading God's Word? Is your mind being changed in character to glorify God, and does that show on your face? Our prayer needs to be that of Psalm 51:10: "Create in me a clean heart O God, and renew a right spirit within me."

Work on memorizing God's Word for the purpose of having your mind transformed and renewed by its power. As you dwell on it, memorize it, and meditate on it, your mind will be transformed and renewed to think more and more on what Colossians 3:2 tells us to do: "Set your minds on things that are above, not on things that are on earth."

Our own willpower is not made of steel. It often fails, and we don't succeed in what we set out to do. Be it dieting, controlling our temper, controlling our tongue, or being more organized, we often don't accomplish what we set out to do. As Paul admitted in Romans 7:15: "For I do not do what I want, but I do the very thing I hate."

How I can relate! How often I say things I regret later. I react before I analyze and before I pray about how I should correctly respond. I have been told: "You have that look on your face," because I am not being careful in some of my external facial reactions. I can blame that on my genes, but my prayer needs to be that I would yield my body, my will, and my mind to the Lord each day.

As we spend time in His Word each day, may we: "Be not conformed to this world, but be transformed by the renewal of your mind, that by testing you may discern what is the will of God, what is good and acceptable and perfect." May our minds be transformed and renewed, growing in the knowledge of God and having a godly mind control. May we dwell more on the things that are above rather than those of this earth.

Listen to: "Fix My Eyes on You," by for KING & COUNTRY.

My thoughts and prayer requests for today are:

NEVER BE SHAKEN

Psalm 62:1–2 (NLT): "I wait quietly before God, for my victory comes from him. He alone is my rock and my salvation, my fortress where I will never be shaken."

I have just returned from the hospital. My husband has had another type of stroke. This is now his second one; the previous one happened three years ago. I wrote my first Bible study book, *Taming the Lion's Roar: Handling Fear in the Midst of a Trial*, after experiencing several serious trials in our life together, and then the culmination came during the stroke that he had in 2012. The doctors now want to know why it has happened again. They are running various tests to find out the "why" to prevent this from happening again. Do I ask God why? No, not anymore. I am sitting in my house, where it is ever so quiet right now. The emergency room was filled with so much noise: police officers, nurses, doctors, lab techs, hospital employees attempting to get your insurance and address information, patients, and people everywhere. Then alarms were going off on various machines that were monitoring oxygen, blood pressure, and other vital signs.

David said in Psalm 62:1–2 that he waited in silence before God. He waited. How do we "wait"? I picture David sitting at the feet of Jesus and not saying anything. He was waiting for God to speak and no one else. God was his help and his shield of protection. David trusted in God and believed that He would surely protect him, because a "fortress" means any place of exceptional security or a strong place. David trusted in God to protect him completely from any harm. God was his fortress.

Psalms 37:7 (NASB) states: "Rest in the LORD and wait patiently for him...." There is something soothing and calming about quietness in contrast to chaotic noise. Look at a sunrise. What sound comes into your mind? Silence. Look at a sunset. What sound picture comes into your mind? Silence. What about when you look up at the dark sky at night, were all of the stars are shining? Silence. God created the sunrise and sunset and the dark sky with the stars brightly shining with all of its majestic beauty, and in contrast we are often worried about how we are going to pay our rent or make the house payment.

Sometimes we just need to listen with all of our might, read God's Word to ourselves out loud, and ask, "Do I get it? Do I hear God speaking to me in the quietness and breathing His Word into my very soul?" Inhale a cleansing breath of God's salvation. Exhale a breath of God's hope and piece.

Wait patiently before God. Be still before Him. He will give you victory. He will rescue you. He will be your rock and your salvation. He will protect you in a strong place, and then you will not be shaken. He will carry you through.

Listen to: "Shoulders," by for KING & COUNTRY.

My thoughts and prayer requests for today are:

_____

_____

_____

_____

_____

_____

_____

_____

_____

_____

_____

_____

_____

_____

_____

_____

_____

_____

_____

SAFETY NET

Psalm 28:7: "The LORD is my strength and my shield; in him my heart trusts, and I am helped, my heart exults, and with my song I give thanks to him."

Right now, as I walk and go through my husband's recovery from his second type of stroke episode, along with a medical emergency for my four-year-old grandson that happened yesterday, I feel like I need a big safety net underneath my feet. I don't feel very sure-footed today.

I read something yesterday by a woman writer where she said that the saying, "This too shall pass," was not biblical. I tend to disagree. I have learned from my past experiences that what is today will not necessarily be tomorrow or a month from now—let alone a year from now. There is an end coming. We all are on a journey of being conformed into Christ's image. Our trials conform us and transform us into what God intends for us to become, which is for us to be molded into being more like Christ.

Think about what protects you from harm and keeps you safe from being hurt. How many items can you come up with that are "shields" in your life? Mine are: sunscreen, seat belts, doctors and medical staff, my regular prescription glasses and my prescription sun glasses, friends, backup for my computer, computer virus software, and even my husband. All of these things help protect me, but how much greater is God's protection and shield over my life for His glory?

God has promised to protect us, shield us, and even defend us. Ecclesiastes 7:12 states: "For the protection of wisdom is like the protection of money, and the advantage of knowledge is that wisdom preserves the life of him who has it." Think about that. Wisdom is a shelter. Wisdom can be a shield and protector from making wrong decisions or even appearing foolish. How I need more wisdom. God has given me His protection as I endure various trials in life, and my confidence is in that fact. I have complete confidence in Psalm 84:11: "For the LORD God is a sun and shield; the LORD bestows favor and honor. No good thing does he withhold from those who walk uprightly."

I will stand up straight. I am taking in a cleansing breath and reciting Psalm 28:7 and inhaling deeply as my ribs expand. Now I am exhaling slowly in a song of praise, giving thanks to my Lord for His protection, found in God's Word and in the prayers of many being provided as the safety net underneath my feet.

My prayer for today is "God give me control over my mind and heart. Let it be controlled by thinking on the things above, where you sit at the right hand of God (Colossians 3:2).

Listen to: "You Are My Strength," by Hillsong.

My thoughts and prayer requests for today are:

_____

_____

_____

_____

_____

_____

_____

_____

_____

_____

_____

_____

_____

_____

_____

_____

_____

_____

TRUST ME

Psalm 25:2: "O my God, in you I trust; let me not be put to shame; let not my enemies exult over me."

Psalm 28:25–26: "But the one who trusts in the LORD will be enriched. Whoever trusts in his own mind is a fool, but he who walks in wisdom will be delivered."

Our four-year-old grandson, Tate, recently had a pretty serious accident that involved him possibly losing a fingernail on one of his little fingers on his left hand. It was an extremely painful incident. Our daughter, Amy, was putting on the new gauze and taping it one evening, and she said to him as he started to be afraid: "Tate, you have to trust Mom. Hold your finger up straight, and I will fix this. You have to trust me! I am not going to hurt you. I am here to take care of you. You have to trust Mom."

Amy's purpose for redoing the gauze-taped bandage was to help keep the fingernail from getting infection and to protect and cushion the wound. What a verbal picture this was to me of how much God loves me and doesn't want to hurt me while I am going through any trial. I have to simply trust Him, just as Tate had to trust his mother to take good care of his injury. God is there to protect me, guard me, and help me, and He will provide His clean and new bandage, keeping my life safe from harm while I undergo any trial. I have to trust Him and have faith that He is working everything out for my good, as it says in Romans 8:28. What a picture this was to me—so simple but so profound!

My grandson had to gather up all of his courage to simply trust in my daughter's love and care for him and know that she was not going to hurt him. He would follow her instruction by taking in a deep breath slowly and then exhaling slowly to get him to calm down and relax. Our cleansing breath comes from breathing in God's promises, allowing us to trust Him, and then exhaling, with His peace flooding our souls. Philippians 4:7 states: "And the peace of God which surpasses all understanding, will guard your hearts and your minds in Christ Jesus." May our minds be guarded today by experiencing and putting into practice heavenly mind control—thinking more on the things above, where Christ is seated at the right hand of God. Our LORD is saying, "Trust me!" "So put your trust in the LORD" (Psalm 4:5)"

Listen to: "Already There," by Casting Crowns.

My thoughts and prayer requests for today are:

SNARE AND DEADFALL TRAPS

Proverbs 13:14: "The teaching of the wise is a fountain of life; that one may turn away from the snares of death."

Proverbs 14:27: "The fear of the LORD is a fountain of life, that one may turn away from the snares of death."

Proverbs 18:7: "A foul's mouth is his ruin, and his lips are a snare to his soul."

2 Timothy 2:26: "And they may come to their senses and escape from the snare of the devil, after captured by him to do his will."

The definition of the word *snare*, when it is used as a noun, is a device that is often consisting of a noose, used for capturing small game. Its purpose is to entrap or entangle unaware. When used as a verb, the definition of *snare* is to catch or involve in trickery.

I found that there are fifteen different best survival snare traps one can purchase or make. There is not just one snare trap, but there are many different kinds to capture various animals. In my research, I found that these are called the best snare and deadfall traps to master. The fifteen different snare traps are: a sharp stick protruding out of the ground with the purpose to puncture an animal's leg; a noose with a bait stick; a motion-activation type with no bait required; various single-use traps; a peg snare trap; a drowning snare; a spring-and-pole snare, called a "treadle snare"; a squirrel-pole snare (preys on the squirrel's love of shortcuts); a rolling snare, which is ideal to use on trails and runs; a figure-four deadfall snare, to be used by trappers; figure-four snare (different from the deadfall snare); a pine pitch bird cup trap; a large rodent trap called a Paiute deadfall; a greasy string deadfall, which is the least complicated snare; a toggle deadfall; and the last one is called a McPhearson spring deadfall. There are snare traps for catching coyotes, hogs, squirrels, rodents, rabbits, and birds and for the purpose of catching food or to get rid of unwanted animals, such as those that are in the rodent family, catching them by surprise, because they are unaware of their downfall.

Some of these traps were very unique. Some appeared very imaginative. Likewise, Satan will be very creative when trying to snare us away from God's truth and get us back into the habit of fear. He will try his best to capture us back into the mode of anxiety and entrap us in fear. He will use many methods: trickery, circumstances, fearful thoughts, lack of trust, lack of faith, lack of self-confidence These will keep us trapped in his snare of guilt, shame, frustration, or feelings of failure. He will change it up from time to time, when we least expect it, to try to make us fall from relying on our Lord and Savior. It won't just be one snare. He has many! What about losing our temper? He just used that one on me yesterday in a situation where I work. Before thinking, I reacted in anger over a mistake I was falsely accused of making. Afterward, I quickly realized that I had just fallen into the enemy's snare, and my response had not been Christlike, and I had to apologize. Or what about the snare of pride? That is another one that can trip me up unknowingly.

Paul warned in 1 Timothy 3:7: "Moreover, he [overseer or elder] must be well thought of by outsiders, so that he may not fall into disgrace, into a snare of the devil." There is that word *snare* again. Satan is after those believers who have had success for the kingdom. Succeeding in our Christlike walk and efforts defeats Satan's power.

Christlikeness has to do with kindness, passionate love of God's Word, loving the body of believers, and seeking to honor Christ. You are now a target. You have defeated his work. You are on the enemy's radar if you are in leadership in ministry, discipling another believer, or simply just trying to not have fear in the trial you are working through once again.

A snare is a trap. Be on guard with the shield of faith to fight against being caught unaware in the snares of sin, discouragement, defeat, fear, pride, and anger. Turn away from the enemy's snares and run straight into the strong tower awaiting you in God's arms. Proverbs 18:10: "The name of the LORD is a strong tower; the righteous man runs into it and is safe."

Listen to: "Forever Reign," by Hillsong.

My thoughts and prayer requests for today are:

WHAT'S NEXT, PAPA?

"This resurrection life you received from God is not a timid, grave-tending life. It's adventurously expectant, greeting God with a childlike, 'What's next, Papa?' God's Spirit touches our spirits and confirms who we really are" (Romans 8:15, MSG).

"God is love…we live in God and God lives in us…. There is no room in love for fear. Well-formed love banishes fear. Since fear is crippling, a fearful life – fear of death, fear of judgment – is one not yet fully formed in love" (1 John 4:18, MSG).

We all face various levels and types of trials in our lives: some experience cancer or other serious health problems; some have wayward family members; some face financial trials—and the list could go on and on. Our heartaches can turn into fear, and that leads to the road of being tormented by anxiety and worry about what might lie ahead. But 2 Timothy 1:7 tells us: "For God has not given us a spirit of fear but of power and love and self-control." So if fearful feelings are not from God, who gives us this feeling of fear? The enemy, not God.

God is perfecting His love in us day by day. If you are His adopted child, if we have accepted Christ as your personal Lord and Savior, then we are preapproved, adopted, chosen children of God! God does not want us to relapse into our old habits of fear when trials occur. We really do not have to fear the past, present, or future, because we have experienced the love of God, and God's love is being perfected in us day by day. God does not take back his forgiveness.

God wants us to live with confidence in His love. Rest in God's love for you. Embrace the fact that God's Spirit lives within you. You are a preapproved child of God. You are being perfected by the love of your heavenly father. The enemy wants to draw you back into the slavery of fear. Fight that and stand firm in God's all-knowing sovereignty. God is in control. He has no limitations. Find perfect peace in knowing that His presence is with you each step of the way. Walk tall, stand up straight, and look forward with a perfect confidence that God is perfecting you in whatever trial you are currently experiencing.

May God be your fortress and refuge in the day of your distress. There will be evidence of maturing in Christ when you can confidently say, "Okay, what's next, Papa?"

Listen to: "Praise You in This Storm," by Casting Crowns.

My thoughts and prayer requests for today are:

DURACELL VS. ENERGIZER®

Ephesians 3:20: "Now to him who is able to do far more abundantly than all that we ask or think; according to the power at work within us."

Ephesians 3:20, KJV: "Now unto him that is able to do exceeding abundantly above all that we ask or think, according to the power that worketh in us."

Ephesians 3:20, NLT: "Now all glory to God, who is able, through his mighty power at work within us, to accomplish infinitely more than we might ask or think."

Paul burst out in this doxology after praying for spiritual strength for the churches around Ephesus. He wanted to display the scope of God's eternal plan for Jews and Gentiles alike. Paul stressed that we are complete in the fullness of God as we grow and learn more about the love of Christ for us—a love that surpasses anything we can understand. Look at these four words in this verse: *all*, *above*, *abundantly*, and *exceeding*. Stop and think about each of those words.

Reread Ephesians 3:20. Now let's examine the definition of *abundance*: more than adequate. A further definition is: "extremely plentiful or over sufficient in quantity or supply."

Whatever you face today, remember this fact: God can do anything far more than you can imagine or guess or even request in your wildest dreams. He does this by working within you deeply and gently. God's power working in you is stronger than any battery you could buy. God is able to do all—exceeding abundantly above all!

Unbelief, doubt, fear, worry, or any unconfessed sin (such as pride) can rob you from your spiritual source of power. Replace these traits with "God confidence." As John 15:5 states: "Without me you can do nothing." God's ability and power is richly abundant, readily available, and above all that we might ask, request, or even think!

Let God be your abundant comforter today. Trust in Him to do far more abundantly than you have prayed about. Recharge your inner battery with Paul's doxology as you are filled with joy and peace and as you put your trust in Him. Ephesians 3:20–21 states: "Now to him who is able to do far more abundantly than all that we ask or think, according to the power at work within us, to him be glory in the church and in Christ Jesus throughout all generations, forever and ever. Amen."

Ask yourself: What does this look like in my life today? May your prayer from today onward be: Lord, I trust you beyond my own understanding. Increase my faith and help my life reflect your infinite grace and mercy. Calm me when I start to tremble. Fill me with your joy and peace as I grasp the fact that you are able to accomplish far more infinitely, abundantly, and over the top of whatever I am asking of you to do today. May I go forth today energized by knowing your infinite power is above and beyond anything I could ask or think of You to do in my life.

Listen to: "The Hurt and the Healer," by MercyMe.

My thoughts and prayer requests for today are:

THE THREE Rs

Philippians 4:4–7: "Rejoice in the Lord always; again I will say, Rejoice. Let your reasonableness be known to everyone. The Lord is at hand. Do not be anxious about anything, but in everything by prayer and supplication with thanksgiving let your requests be made known to God, and the peace of God, which surpasses all understanding, will guard your hearts and your minds in Christ Jesus."

My natural reflex tendency when experiencing a trial or burden is not necessarily calmness and tranquility. My pulse races. I have shallow breathing. I tend to sigh a lot to try to release the pressure I am feeling. Then the stress in my body often goes to my neck, which becomes extremely tight and often painful, and it may turn into a migraine headache, requiring another trip to my chiropractor to get my neck readjusted. But Paul gave the formula to the church in Philippi, in Philippians 4:4-7, to combat the problem of anxiety. It still works today. Chuck Swindoll once said to replace anxiety with the three Rs: rejoice in God's power, relax in the Lord, and rest in the Lord's protection and provision. This is so true!

Rejoice. Rejoice in the many previous answers to prayers you have had. In Philippians 4:4, Paul says not once but twice: "Rejoice!" Draw upon past answers to prayers and spend time thanking God for each one of them. Psalm 32:11 declares: "Be glad in the LORD, and rejoice, O righteous, and shout for joy, all you upright in heart!"

Have you ever shouted for joy? Try it! Do you remember Psalm 118:24, which was also a song I sang as a child? "This is the day that the LORD has made; let us rejoice and be glad in it." Then there is the song we sing at Christmastime: "Rejoice! Rejoice! Emanuel shall come to thee, oh Israel!" I wonder why we only sing that at Christmastime. Spend some time rejoicing and singing praise and worship to the Lord and watch those anxious feelings start to lessen.

Get alone with God and spend time worshipping Him. Guard your mind from spending too much time watching TV and spend more time reading good books written by Christian authors and teachers. Reboot your mind toward heavenly things.

Relax. Does it take work to relax? When you have turned over everything to God by praying with adoration and a humble and submissive heart and mind, then take a "pause." After you have thanked God for all He has done, you will have peace.

What does *reasonableness* mean in Philippians 4:5? It means showing patience, gentleness, generosity, goodwill, friendliness, and graciousness. It involves showing charity toward the faults of others, mercy toward the faults of others, and indulgence of the failures of others. Let it go. Ouch. This is often hard for me to do. Yet it sums up what having real contentment is all about. In the VOICE, Philippians 4:5 reads like this: "Keep your gentle nature so that all men may know what it looks like to walk in His footsteps." In other words: relax!

Rest. Now rest in the Lord's protection. Worry about nothing. Pray about everything. Model peace instead of panic and fear.

Psalm 23:2 states: "He makes me lie down in green pastures, He leads me beside still waters." Isn't a picture of lush green pastures and a view of the ocean calming, soothing, and restful? Did you know that the brain heals itself while the body is sleeping and is at rest?

Pray about everything. Let God's peace flood your inner soul. Get the sleep that God intended you to have. God never sleeps. He's on watch 24/7. He's got this!

Listen to: "Carry Me Now," by Josh Wilson.

My thoughts and prayer requests for today are:

OFF BALANCE

Psalm 94:18–19: "When I thought 'My foot slips,' your steadfast love, O LORD, held me up. When the cares of my heart are many, your consolations cheer my soul."

When my husband had his second stroke, he lost balance on the left side of his body. He had trouble standing on only one foot and would tend to fall over when asked by the hospital's physical therapist to stand in this position. He had to do various exercises intended to increase his balance in order to strengthen his sure-footed ability to regain his balance. The exercises worked in a close relationship with the healing process.

This was the picture that came to my mind in Psalm 94:18 when David said that his leg or foot "slips." The Hebrew meaning for the word *ma-ta*(h)—"slips"—in this verse literally means to sway, totter, or swagger. Being off balance and feeling like you are going to fall down is an uncomfortable feeling. But the Lord's faithfulness, mercy, and steadfast love support us. He gives us strength and sustains us so we can go forward again and not fall down into the enemy's trap of anxious thoughts or temptations.

Notice the word *cares* in verse 19: "When the cares of my heart are many…." It is plural. When the anxious and disturbing cares derail us and doubts fill our mind, God's comfort gives us renewed hope: "Your consolations cheer my soul."

The word *consolations* is plural as well, meaning that there is more than one consolation given to us by the Lord to cheer our souls! God's faithfulness, mercy, support, and strength uplift our souls.

Draw close to God and let that connection fill your soul with peace and joy. Let God extinguish any heaviness of heart with His divine and abundant comfort and consolations, holding you up to stand firm, stand upright in total confidence of not being off balance. Cling to the truths in Psalm 94:22: "But the LORD has become my stronghold, and my God the rock of my refuge."

Lastly, Philippians 4:1 declares: "Therefore, my brothers, whom I love and long for, my joy and crown, stand firm thus in the Lord my beloved." Stand upright, stand up straight, and don't stumble into Satan's traps of derailment. Stand firm in the Lord. Draw upon God's consolations and in His faithful love for you. Have them embedded into your mind from His Word. Go forth with sure footing on your path, with one foot ahead of the other, step by step.

Listen to: "Day by Day (and with Each Passing Moment)," sung by Katherine Journey (which can be found on Into the Light Journal's YouTube Channel).

My thoughts and prayer requests for today are:

BE QUICK AND BE SLOW

James 1:19–20: "Know this, my beloved brothers: let every person be quick to hear, slow to speak, slow to anger; for the anger of man does not produce the righteousness of God."

James is sometimes called: "the Proverbs of the New Testament." Oh how practical this verse is in reminding us how to control not only what comes out of our mouths but how it comes out of our mouths and is received.

Have you developed good listening skills, or do you prefer to be the talker? My husband graciously pointed out to me recently that I was interrupting and finishing sentences with a couple we were visiting with. He said, "Linda, what you say is important, but you need to wait your turn!"

James says that we need to be quick to hear. Romans 10:17 states: "So faith comes from hearing, and hearing through the word of Christ." We must first be good listeners before reacting in our own speech. Someone once said that effective communicators are good listeners. Watch yourself today: Do you have the quality of listening to others thoroughly without finishing their sentences? The next time you disagree with someone, first truly listen to what they are saying and how they are saying it. Is he or she hurt? Is he or she angry?

Why? When you are sitting there being the sincere listener, your mouth is shut while the other person spews out his or her words. Maybe the other person doesn't want your opinion and just needs you to be the listener. That is being "quick to hear," which is what James says is important. Likewise, we need to be quick to hear what God is saying to us each day.

After thoroughly hearing and understanding what is being said, then pause. James says next that we should be slow to speak. Oh how I need to think through my thoughts first before having those words of reaction come out! Too many times I regret what I have said and wish that I could take back words or wish that I had thought through my words better before speaking. Do you ever have those regrets?

Finally, we are only to be quick to hear and then slow to speak, but James finishes by saying that we are to be slow to get angry. Ouch! That is not my natural response.

James's order of response sounds like a dance step: quick, slow, slow; quick, slow, slow. We must be: quick to hear and obey God; slow to speak, since Proverbs 17:28 tells us: "Even a fool who keeps silent is considered wise; when he closes his lips, he is deemed intelligent"; and lastly, we need to be slow in losing our tempers or in speaking harshly.

May we listen twice as much as we speak, since it is true that God has given us two ears and only one mouth. Quick, slow, slow. May we portray intelligence and wisdom before looking like fools.

Quick, slow, slow.

Listen to: "Live Like That," by Sidewalk Prophets.

My thoughts and prayer requests for today are:

WHAT I DON'T KNOW AND DO KNOW

James 4:14: "Yet you do not know what tomorrow will bring. What is your life? For you are a mist that appears for a little time and then vanishes."

Isn't Google a wonderful tool for looking up answers to questions? When I was a child, we had a set of *World Book* encyclopedias, which were considered the best a person could buy at that time. The alphabetically arranged books contained information on just about everything. We used them to complete our research papers and homework. Now we have Google on our computers and smartphones, and we can quickly and easily get answers to just about everything. However, there are some questions for which Google cannot provide the answers: What about my future? What is the outcome of this medical condition for me? How long will the recovery take in my case, my friend's case, or my husband's case? What decision should I make in this hard situation in my life?

I don't know what tomorrow will bring, but I know the following:

- By drawing near to God, He will draw near to me. I am to submit to God, resist the devil, and he will flee from me – James 4:7–8.

- If I humble myself before the Lord, He will exalt me – James 4:10.
- God knows the plans He has for me. His plans for me are for my good and not for evil, to give me a hope and a future with Him – Jeremiah 29:11.
- My citizenship is in heaven – Philippians 3:20–21.

I do not know if a church member's cancer will show up again on the scan that was done today. I do not know how long my husband will have double vision in his left eye. I do not know when the discs in my back will flare up with problems again and hinder me in walking. I do not know the outcomes of various scenarios, but I know that God loves me, has chosen me, and has accepted me. One day I will walk the streets of gold, living in a mansion prepared for me, where there will be no more tears and no more pain. That I *do* know!

James 4:14, NLT: "How do you know what your life will be like tomorrow? Your life is like the morning fog—it's here a little while, then it is gone."

During my teenage years there was song that was often sung before the Sunday morning sermon during the "special music" spot: "I Know Who Holds Tomorrow." The words go through my head often. As you listen to this song, may it remind you that we don't know about tomorrow or seem to understand, but we know that God holds our future, and we know that God holds our hand!

What things are you struggling with that you just don't know the outcome for or the answers to? God knows. Trust Him.

Listen to: "I Know Who Holds Tomorrow," as sung by Kelly Price.

My thoughts and prayer requests for today are:

TEMPORARY RESIDENCE

1 Peter 1:17 (HCSB): "And if you address as Father, the One who judges impartially based on each one's work, you are to conduct yourselves in fear during the time of your temporary residence."

Think about our "temporary residence" on this earth as Christians. The KJV uses the word *sojourning*, which means, again, a temporary stay or short visit. First Peter 2:11 continues this thought by stating: "Dear friends, I urge you as *strangers and temporary residents* to abstain from fleshly desires that war against you" (emphasis mine).

This earth is simply my temporary residence. Someday my address will be heaven. John MacArthur said, "Your inside lives in heaven and your outside lives here. Live the risen life." As Colossians 3:2 tells us: "Set your minds on things that are above, not on things that are on the earth."

Heavenly mind control is about setting our minds on our eternal destiny and reward as believers. Eternity is our reward, and we will get to share in God's glory. I must remember the words on the little plaque that is on the wall in my garage: "Perhaps today!" We must train our minds to look at earthly things through heaven's point of view. Earth is our temporary residence, and we must conduct ourselves in holy reverence and obedience to our heavenly Father.

Christ could come back for us today! We are simply residing in our temporary residence.

Temporary residence. Sojourning stay. Perhaps today!

Listen to: "This World Is Not My Home," recorded by various artists, and also listen to: "There Will Be a Day," by Jeremy Camp.

My thoughts and prayer requests for today are:

JUST OBEDIENCE

1 Peter 1:22: "Having purified your souls by your obedience to the truth for a sincere brotherly love, love one another earnestly from a pure heart."

1 Peter 1:22, NLT: "You were cleansed from your sins when you obeyed the truth, so now you must show sincere love to each other as brothers and sisters. Love each other deeply with all your heart."

1Peter 1:22, MSG: "Now that you've cleaned up your lives by following the truth, love one another as if your lives depended on it. Your new life is not like your old life."

Peter tells us that we are to love one another earnestly and from a pure heart. It must be a sincere love. This type of love is a choice and must be stretched to the limits. Only we who are Christians have the ability and capacity within us to love like this. Furthermore, when we love sincerely and earnestly, we are performing obedience to what God has commanded us to do. As He said in John 15:12, "This is my commandment, that you love one another as I have loved you."

But why do we women have such a hard time with unity and getting along? We are given an actual example in Philippians 4:2–3 of two women who had this very problem. It caused disruption and division within the church, and it had to be handled. Paul said: "I entreat Euodia and I entreat Syntyche to agree in the Lord. Yes, I ask you also, true companion, help these women, who have labored side by side with me in the gospel together with Clement and the rest of my fellow workers, who names are in the book of life." Even the Apostle Paul saw women not getting along in ministry and recorded it for us to be aware of and learn from.

The commandment to love one another appears throughout the Bible. It comes up again and again, as it does in today's verse from 1 Peter 1:22.

Perhaps you're thinking, "But, do you know what she said to me?" Yes, I do. I have seen this happen wherever I have lived. Let it go. Warren Wiersbe said it so well: "You would think that those who walk in hope and holiness would be able to walk in harmony, but this is not always true."

John 13:35 states: "By this all people will know that you are my disciples, if you have love for one another." Our love for one another in the body of Christ is a testimony to the world. I often explain to people that when I go to my church, it is like getting a big hug! People are excited to be there, and it shows on their faces!

So today I choose to show sincere love to my brothers and sisters in the Lord and to love each of them deeply with all my heart. We need to display unity and togetherness within the body of Christ. No excuses. Just obedience.

Listen to: "Thrive," by Casting Crowns.

My thoughts and prayer requests for today are:

DILIGENTLY STAYING ON COURSE

Psalm 119:1–4, MSG: "You're blessed when you stay on course, walking steadily on the road revealed by God. You're blessed when you follow his directions, doing your best to find him. That's right – you don't go off on your own; you walk straight along the road he set. You, God, prescribed the right way to live; now you expect us to live it. Oh that my steps might be steady, keeping to the course you set."

Psalm 119:4 "You have commanded your precepts to be kept diligently."

We are to keep on keeping on, following God, and not straying from the truth of His Word in our lives. We are to stay on the path where God wants us to live. The enemy will throw torpedoes and every kind of distraction our way to try to keep us from living out a godly testimony. But we must remain steadfast. When verse one talks about "walking steadily," it refers to a habitual pattern of living. Our integrity must be a light to others as we follow God's instructions. My pastor, Todd Smith, just said this morning: "Integrity—mean what you say, and do what you promise."

Scripture tells us that when we stay on course for God, we are blessed. Other verses throughout Psalm 119 declare that Scripture is more valuable than money. For example, look at verse 14: "In the way of your testimonies I delight as much as in all riches." Verse 72 also says: "The law of your mouth is better to me than thousands of gold and silver pieces." Do you value God's Word more than material possessions?

When we follow God's directions we are staying on course and gain eternal blessings. When we walk in the path of God's commandments, we reflect Christlikeness.

The psalmist was passionate about desiring to obey God's Word. He used the word *diligently* (ESV). Diligence means not giving up and working hard; not getting distracted and being focused. In Psalm 119:101–102 he says, "I hold back my feet from every evil way, in order to keep your word. I do not turn aside from your rules, for you have taught me." That is diligently staying on course.

Diligently keep your feet on the road God has revealed. Diligently live for God. Diligently work at living for God. Stay focused in your growing relationship with the LORD. Walk straight: head up, shoulders back; inhale deeply and then exhale slowly. Look up!

Listen to: "Fix My Eyes," by for KING & COUNTRY.

My thoughts and prayer requests for today are:

_____

_____

_____

_____

_____

_____

_____

_____

_____

_____

_____

_____

_____

_____

_____

_____

_____

_____

_____

_____

_____

A. S. K.

Luke 11:9: "And I tell you, ask, and it will be given to you; seek, and you will find; knock, and it will be opened to you."

A – Ask God specifically for what you need. Be direct. Keep on asking, and you will receive it if it is God's will for Him to give it to you. It may not be this very minute, but His answer will either be no, not at all; no, not now; or yes, but in His sovereign timing.

S – Seek Him with all your heart, soul, and mind. Keep on seeking Him, and you will find your answer through His Word.

K – Knock, and the door will be opened.

When you ask you will receive. When you seek God, you will find what you need from reading and meditating on Scripture. The door will be opened to everyone who knocks at their heavenly father's door. When your children ask you for something specifically, don't you want to give it to them (within reason, of course)?

Keep on keeping on. Keep on asking. Keep on seeking. Keep praying and seeking God's wisdom and direction. Keep on knocking. Come to God continually and not just during emergencies. First Thessalonians 5:17 commands: "Pray without ceasing." Only God is able to control the circumstances, and He is working things out behind the scenes that you can't even see or don't even know.

Keep having a heavenly mind-set, and don't let problems deter your efforts to keep your mind focused on heavenly things. As it says in Colossians 3:1–2: "Seek the things that are above, where Christ is seated at the right hand of God. Set your minds on things that are above, not on things that are on earth." Keep seeking the light.

Ask. Seek. Knock. God will meet your need! There is a new day coming!

Listen to: "Pushing Back the Dark," by Josh Wilson.

My thoughts and prayer requests for today are:

BUCKLE UP!

Ephesians 6:11, 13: "Put on the whole armor of God, that you may be able to stand against the schemes of the devil. Therefore take up the whole armor of God, that you may be able to withstand in the evil day, and having done all, to stand firm."

Do you have all of your armor on to withstand the devil's bullets today? What is his scheme to make you to trip up today? Where are you vulnerable to such attacks? The word *scheme* means a plan of action, an underhanded plot, and, in this case, always full of deception. The devil will use every crafty sin, immoral and false theology, and worldly enticement to catch us up in one of his schemes. He will pervert God's Word and hinder the gospel, as he prevented Paul, a servant of Christ, from coming to the church at Thessalonica (1 Thessalonians 2:18). He blinds the minds of unbelievers (1 Corinthians 4:4), plots against those in ministry leadership to fall in disgrace (1 Timothy 4:7), and last but not least, as 1 John 4:4 declares: "Little children, you are from God and have overcome them, for he who is in you is greater than he who is in the world." We must be aware of false teaching and be sharpened by the Holy Spirit, as he will always lead us to sound doctrine and the assurance that no one can take a believer out of God's hands. God's power overcomes the devil's power.

So we must put on the whole armor of God to withstand the various schemes of attack against us. Fasten on your "belt of truth" (Ephesians 6:14). The belt signified a soldier synching up his robe so that it didn't hinder him from being ready to fight and in order for him to be able to run into battle quickly. We must quickly and alertly be ready to fight the devil's schemes against us with the truth of God's Word. With integrity and a clear conscience, we can face the enemy without fear. The soldier's belt also held his sword. We must use the Word of God, our sword of defense, to combat Satan's lies.

The next piece of armor mentioned is the "breastplate of righteousness." The breastplate covered a soldier's full body, protecting his heart and other vital organs—front and back. This symbolizes the believer's righteousness in Christ. Our chief protection against the devil's schemes is living a righteous and holy life, which is the very character of God Himself. We must live faithfully in righteous obedience and communion with Christ, or we will be open to Satan's attack.

The shoes of the gospel (Ephesians 6:15) are the next articles of armor to wear. Warren Wiersbe said that the most victorious Christian is a witnessing Christian. Take the gospel with you wherever you go.

Ephesians 6:16 talks about the "shield of faith." The soldier's shield protected him from spears, arrows, and flaming darts. The shields were constructed so that they interlocked with other soldiers' shields. That way they could form a complete line of defense against the enemy and march into the enemy as a solid wall. What are the devil's darts thrown that he throws at us? They are blasphemous thoughts, hateful thoughts about others, doubts, and burning desires for sin. We never know when a temptation will hit us, so we must always walk by faith and use the "shield of faith" to daily live out our faith in God through his promises and his power. Faith is the defensive weapon that will protect us against the schemes of the enemy.

How does the "helmet of salvation," which is named in Ephesians 6:17, keep us safe? Satan wants to attack our minds. Satan wants to deceive us with doubts about our salvation. When God controls our minds, Satan cannot lead us astray. Satan wants to deceive us with doubts, but our security in Christ is a fact.

The last piece of armor to put on is found in Ephesians 6:17: "…and the sword of the Spirit, which is the Word of God." The Word of God pierces the heart. When we use our sword, which is the Scriptures, against Satan, he will be crippled and stopped. Satan will try to confuse us, as he did with Eve in the garden. The better you know the Word of God, the better you will be able to withstand this scheme of attacks against you from the enemy.

Do you have your armor on? The enemy will start his attack when you are the most vulnerable. Know where you are the most vulnerable. Have you had a lack of sleep? Are you struggling with an issue? Are you making a difference in God's kingdom? Put on, fasten, and buckle up the whole armor of God as Ephesians 6:13 says: "Therefore take up the whole armor of God, that you may be able to withstand in the evil day, and having done all, to stand firm."

Put on: The belt of truth, breastplate of righteousness, shoes of the gospel, shield of faith, helmet of salvation, and the sword of the Spirit. Now you are ready and equipped to fight today's battles!

Listen to: "Keep Fighting the Good Fight," by Chad Mattson.

My thoughts and prayer requests for today are:

NEVER ON HOLD

Ephesians 6:18: "Praying at all times in the Spirit, with all prayer and supplication. To that end keep alert with all perseverance, making supplication for all the saints."

Our prayer life is supposed to be in a continual flow of communication with the Lord. We can pray while we are driving, cooking, doing laundry, cleaning, dusting, vacuuming, gardening, exercising, etc. "Praying at all times" means all the time, which means frequently, not just when disaster hits. Prayer is the power to gain victory and defeat Satan, and it is the glue that holds our armor together.

Praying at all times is like leaving your computer or smartphone on and never turning it off. It is ready to go at all times. When we are praying and talking to God, he never puts us on hold. We never have to wait for him to pick up a phone and take our call or call us back. Just think, our prayers never go to voice mail! Do you realize that you have never left His presence? He is right there all the time. We must be constantly in prayer, because we are always under various temptations or attacks from the devil.

As you are praying, don't forget to praise God and give words of thanksgiving from a thankful heart. Praise can change one's attitude into joy and peace. We have both wants and desires in our requests. Our wants are not always our needs. Is your most important prayer right now a need to be met or a desire to be fulfilled?

Be an intercessor for others. When you tell someone you are going to pray for him or her, write it down and be sure to pray. Keep that commitment. "Making supplication for all the saints" (Ephesians 6:18).

Keep alert when you are praying. I have a folding chair in my office, which is where I have my morning time with God. I have a paper on this chair that says: "God's Chair." That helps me be more personal in my prayer conversation with God. It helps me realize that He is sitting right there, and I can tell Him anything. He will never say, "You told me that already." Don't give up on praying for a particular desire or need. Persevere. Keep praying until God answers. Warren Wiersbe said that just about the time you feel like quitting, God will give the answer.

Even Paul asked believers to pray for him. Paul didn't ask for comfort or even for safety, but he prayed that he would be an effective witness in his ministry. Pray for your church staff and your pastor and elders to be effective. Pray that they will be infused with true knowledge received from God's Word. Pray for family and friends to become passionate about God's Word so they will be obedient and faithful to God. Ask the Lord to open up your mind to understand the knowledge and true meaning of His Word and not just someone else's opinion. Ask the Holy Spirit to give you His full knowledge so that you will be able to apply it to your life.

Pray all the time. It never has to be formal. Keep your mind on heavenly things as it says in Colossians 3:1–2, NLT: "Set your sights on the realities of heaven, where Christ sits in the place of honor at God's right hand. Think about the things of heaven, not the things of earth."

But what does it mean to "pray in the Spirit?" This has really stumped me. This has been a challenge to me as I have asked God, "What does it mean to pray in the Spirit? Lord, I want to pray in the Spirit." It says in Romans 8:26–27: "Likewise the Spirit helps us in our weakness. For we do not know what to pray for as we ought, but the Spirit himself intercedes for us with groaning's too deep for words. And he who searches hearts knows what is the mind of the Spirit, because the Spirit intercedes for the saints according to the will of God."

To pray in the Spirit is the most important thought Paul gave about praying. It is not something dramatic or overly ecstatic in nature. We are to pray in Jesus's name as He said in John 14:13: "If you ask me anything in my name I will do it." We are to pray for things consistent with His will.

John MacArthur says that to be "filled with the Spirit" (Ephesians 5:18) and to walk in His leading and power is to be made able to pray in the Spirit, because our prayer will then be in harmony with His. As we submit to the Holy Spirit, obeying His Word and relying on His leading and strength, we will be drawn into close and deep fellowship with the Father and the Son. This is a simple definition of what it means to pray in the Spirit.

Praying in the Spirit is an admission of a believer's ignorance and his or her dependence on God. We must persevere in praying without ceasing, giving praise and thanks to God and not giving in to discouragement.

Keep alert, keep on praying, and pray for others. Submit to the Holy Spirit. Obey His Word. Rely on the Holy Spirit's leading and strength. Be still. Listen.

Listen to: "Strong Enough," by Matthew West, and "Closer to Love," by Mat Kearny.

My thoughts and prayer requests for today are:

INEVITABLE

1 Peter 1:6–7: "In this you rejoice, though now for a little while, if necessary, you have been grieved by various trials, so that the tested genuineness of your faith—more precious than gold that perishes though it be tested by fire—may be found to result in praise and glory and honor at the revelation of Jesus Christ."

Trials are inevitable. As my pastor, Todd Smith, says: "You are either going into a trial or coming out of a trial." Practicing a heavenly mind-set and heavenly mind control involves realizing that God is preparing us for what is ahead for us in heaven. Trials are some of God's tools, and they are the manuals for the school of wisdom and experience so that we can, in turn, comfort and help others. Peter was speaking here about the general problems Christians face as they are surrounded by unbelievers.

Sometimes trials are for discipline because of our lack of obedience. David said in Psalm 119:67: "Before I was afflicted I went astray, but now I keep your word." At other times, trials help us grow spiritually or prevent us from sinning (1 Corinthians 12:7–8). There will be many trials (plural) in our lives.

The trials I have gone through have produced grief and pain, which is inevitable. But, trials do not last forever. As someone has said:

"When God permits His children to go through the furnace, He keeps His eye on the clock and His hand on the thermostat." God is always in control. He wants us to seek Him with all of our heart, soul, and mind. Our trials help mold us into knowing God at a more intimate level in our relationship with Him.

A goldsmith would keep the metal in the furnace until he could see his face reflected on the metal. Our Lord will keep us in a furnace of suffering until we reflect the glory and beauty of Jesus Christ. Our successes in life don't always teach us lessons, but our mistakes do.

You may not be able to rejoice in your trial today, but you can rejoice in what is ahead in heaven. That is what keeping a heavenly mind-set is all about (Colossians 3:1–4).

I have often felt strong empathy for Job. Job went through painful trials that God allowed in his life. "But he knows the way that I take; when he has tried me, I shall come out as gold" (Job 23:10). Do you feel you are golden in color sometimes due to a succession of several trials or maybe a big trial you are going through? I have felt that way.

What will you do about that trial? Ask God to help strengthen your faith. Ask Him what he wants you to learn. God is orchestrating the events in our lives. Give praise and glory to God, knowing that this world is not our home, and heaven is. There is an end and an outcome to every trial. It does not last forever. Stand firm in your commitment and have assurance that Christ is sufficient in all things. You are complete in Him. Give praise, glory, and honor to Him, fully knowing that Christ may return today. Be ready!

For further Bible study on this subject, go through my Bible study book, *Taming the Lion's Roar: Handling Fear in the Midst of a Trial.*

Listen to: "Know by Now," by Josh Wilson.

My thoughts and prayer requests for today are:

LIVING THE LIFE

I realized recently while soaking in a historical decision being made for our country, that Peter nailed it back in 1 Peter 2:11–12 when he said: "Beloved I urge you as sojourners and exiles to abstain from the passions of the flesh, which wage war against your soul. Keep your conduct among the Gentiles honorable, so that when they speak against you as evildoers, they may see your good deeds and glorify God on the day of visitation." I like how the HCSB words verse 11: "Dear friends, I urge you as strangers and temporary residents to abstain from fleshly desires that war against you." Once again, Peter reminds us that this world is our temporary address, just as he did in 1 Peter 1:17. Christ is coming again to take us to our eternal home in heaven, and I can see that it is getting closer and closer to that day!

Peter stressed that there was a spiritual battle going on against us. How we live always speaks volumes to others. Two separate times I have had individuals within my work contacts tell me that they knew me from when they worked for their previous employers. I have no recollection of them, but they remember me, which is frightening. I couldn't help but wonder if my conduct was a testimony to these individuals or not.

As Christian women, we need to have an impact on those we come into contact with in our work, our community, our church, and our families. I often wonder what I will be remembered for when I pass on to glory? Will gentleness be a quality I am remembered for? Other admirable qualities would be that I was lovely, gracious, noble, excellent, and disciplined in maintaining joy and peace when disagreements arose. These are the qualities I so admire in others and want to have them exemplified in my life.

Unsaved people are watching us and so often keep a higher standard for us than we even do for ourselves. There must be nothing in our conduct that will give them ammunition to attack Christ or the gospel. Our daily life must back up what we profess to believe. We are all soldiers in a spiritual battle. Peter used the word *war* in verse 11, regarding sinful passions that we will need to fight against. We face a constant warfare to fight against. We need to be on guard. We must exemplify purity while living in a sinful world. Our integrity must be proof of our Christian faith.

Remember, somebody's watching you today, whether you realize it or not! What impression will you leave to bring Christ glory? Continue to keep your mind on heavenly things so that your conduct will stand as a witness for Christ.

Listen to: "We Fall Down," by Kutless.

My thoughts and prayer requests for today are:

_____

_____

_____

_____

_____

_____

_____

_____

_____

_____

_____

_____

_____

_____

_____

_____

_____

_____

_____

_____

A FREE GIFT—490 TIMES

I realized while reading 1 Peter 3:9–11 that forgiveness is a free gift I can give to those who offend me or who hurt my feelings. When I am made to feel not quite good enough, I can give something that does not cost me any money, which is forgiveness. It will not deplete my bank account. Look at what Peter says:

> Do not repay evil for evil or reviling for reviling, but on the contrary, bless, for to this you were called, that you may obtain a blessing. For Whoever desires to love life and see good days, let him keep his tongue from evil and his lips from speaking deceit; let him turn away from evil and do good; let him seek peace and pursue it (1 Peter 3:9–11).

Why is this so hard for us women to do—to forgive when the other person isn't asking us to forgive him or her? Why is it so easy to hold a grudge and keep remembering past offenses, rather than simply offering forgiveness seventy times seven, which, if you do the math, equals 490 times! Peter says that we are called to bless others so that we may obtain a blessing. I want more blessings, don't you? God has graciously bestowed forgiveness upon me and has given me undeserved blessings instead of judgment. Why doesn't that come to mind first instead of my feeling offended and that old sin nature of bitterness waging war against me? Why is giving a blessing not my first reflex after being hurt? Why do I, instead, let my mind concentrate on words that hurt me?

Peter says that we are called to bless. It also says this in Luke 6:38: "Give, and it will be given to you." In the Old Testament, Leviticus 19:18 states: "You shall not take vengeance or bear a grudge against the sons of your own people, but you shall love your neighbor as yourself: I am the LORD." There it is: God commanded us not to hold a grudge!

I must turn away from holding onto any grudges. I am commanded to bless others. I must guard my tongue from slandering others who have hurt me. I must guard my mouth against sarcasm in retaliation. Ouch. I must make sure that I have my armor on and not allow Satan to attack me where I am vulnerable simply because I do not have a forgiving spirit. Peter ends with: "seek peace and pursue it." Forgiving others is a free gift and will enable us to love life and see good days. Keep a humble, loving attitude. The NLT says in 1 Peter 3:9 not to retaliate with insults when others insult you. Instead, pay them back with a blessing. In fact, that is what God has called us to do.

Forgiveness is a gift that you don't even have to put in a box and gift wrap. It is free to give. Be a blessing. That is your job: to bless. And when you do, you will obtain a blessing from God.

Listen to: "Forgiven," by Sanctus Real.

My thoughts and prayer requests for today are:

_____
_____
_____
_____
_____
_____
_____
_____
_____
_____
_____
_____
_____
_____
_____
_____
_____
_____
_____

GIVING A BLESSING

I have been thinking about how we are to bless others freely. This is what God has called us to do—bless others. First Peter 4:10–11 states: "As each has received a gift, use it to serve one another, as good stewards of God's varied grace: whoever speaks, as one who speaks oracles of God; whoever serves, as one who serves by the strength that God supplies—in order that in everything God may be glorified through Jesus Christ."

Peter said in 1 Peter 4:10–11 that we each have received a gift, and we are to use it to serve one another. Spiritual gifts are to be used for showing loving concern for the benefit of others and to glorify God in the process. John MacArthur said that Peter was implying that there were two kinds of gifts: speaking gifts and serving gifts. Each of these gifts is needed.

Be aware of other people's gifts and "love languages" (Be sure to read the book: *The 5 Love Languages*, by Gary Chapman, for more information on this topic.). Serve others in that way, and you will give them a blessing by giving your gift to them. First Peter 4:11 (HCSB) states: "If anyone speaks, it should be as one who speaks God words; if anyone serves it should be from the strength God provides, so that God maybe glorified through Jesus Christ in everything." Oh how I pray that I will be speaking God words to people I come in contact with or to those who read this devotional book!

My mind was recently very bothered about how I was going to be able to fulfill a financial situation. I didn't know what the dollar amount would be, but I could see that it would be substantial and maybe cause a door to close that I had been praying about for months. How in the world was I going to be able to afford a burning desire that I had prayed about and had set out to do? I gathered up all my courage and posed the question in an e-mail. To my surprise, the reply from the person on the other end spoke God words to me! My love tank was brimming over! The other person replied with only two sentences! But the words immediately zinged in my heart, and I was immediately humbled and filled with immense gratitude!

The Holy Spirit reminded me of God's promise in Ephesians 3:20 that says: "Now to him who is able to do far more abundantly than all that we ask or think...." This was it! God was giving me a blessing! This person was giving me a blessing, and it was just like I received a big Christmas present early! The words she wrote—her God words—ministered to my love language: "words of affirmation" (taken from Gary Chapman's book that I mentioned above). I was dancing around our bedroom, shouting praise to the Lord! My arms were lifted up in praises of gratitude and filled with overflowing joy to the gracious goodness God gave to me! I am keeping the e-mail and not deleting it!

I actually have an e-mail my Dad sent me last year that I have not deleted. His words of affirmation and encouragement to me regarding my Bible study book, *Taming the Lion's Roar: Handling Fear in the Midst of a Trial*, filled up my love tank! My Dad was a high school teacher and taught Sunday school classes at our home church for years. I remember that he took a college class in writing one summer. For him to give me this compliment spoke volumes to me and was a special gift.

Now the question is, who can I speak God's words to today? Who can I give a blessing to today? Ask yourself who can be blessed by you in that text or e-mail or phone call today. If you are more of a behind-the-scenes person, who needs your act of service today? Someone is just waiting and yearning to get a blessing from another sister in Christ. We must be sensitive to being in tune with the Holy Spirit's promptings, telling us who we need to reach out to today. Additionally, we must be good managers of the spiritual gifts God has so graciously given to each of us for His glory. May we be filling up our sisters' love tanks!

Listen to: "Pouring It out for You," by the Newsboys.

My thoughts and prayer requests for today are:

GIVE ME JOY!

In 2010, my husband and I went through two or three deep financial trials. It was hard to understand why it happened, which is usually the case when someone goes through deep, deep times of trouble. I was experiencing many panic attacks regarding one of the situations in particular. I was extremely disappointed by the failed expectations of what seemed to be a sound investment—but it turned out otherwise.

Then there was a separate situation where we had to trust God completely for his righteous justice, and not our, to be put into place. I had many days of deep depression. But then, one morning as I was pleading with the Lord to give me joy, I read Psalm 25 and started to write out my request and thoughts on paper as I met and talked with Him. This was what came out of that morning's conversation:

GIVE ME JOY!

Give me joy, exhilarating joy.
Give me joy abounding in increased faith in You.
Give me joy so my laughter can be heard and seen.
Give me joy from knowing You and believing in You.
Give me joy from finding satisfaction in You.
Give me joy from Your peace.
Give me joy from spending time in Your presence.

You are my rock.
You are my strength.
Your cross holds me up for my future with You in eternity.
You are my encourager so I may be a light to others.

You have helped me increase my faith in You, which gives me joy.
You have given me new things to laugh about, which makes me joyful.
You have given me friends, relationships, and wisdom that I may shine forth in exhilarating joy!
You have confided in me when I cried out and sought your guidance and answers so that I may have joy.
You have given me joy in knowing Jesus!

Listen to: "To You O Lord I Lift Up My Soul (Psalm 25)," by Graham Kendrick.

My thoughts and prayer requests for today are:

APHIDS

Today we discovered, much to our horror, that in our beautiful homemade greenhouse, aphids were all over our spinach and radish plants. It was not a pretty sight. Growing fresh vegetables and herbs has been such a wonderful experience and has added great salads full of vitamin K at our dinner table. I got out a sample of my company's formula of a potassium cocoate liquid soap concentrate and added it to a spray bottle of water. I sprayed all of the plants and those aphids. I came back a of couple hours later and doused them all again. They were still there, and a few were actively crawling on the leaves of the radishes. I was going to have to explore other options in my fight over these aphids.

As I write this, we are currently in a drought in Southern California. We are only allowed to have our lawn sprinklers on two days a week. Grass is not very green in our "awesome town" community (that is the slogan on the billboard when you enter our community). Many lawns are dry and brown. However, the forecast says that this fall will bring a huge amount of rain, which is called El Niño. Residents and businesses are having to replace some plants with succulents and other landscape options.

The aphids and my spots of brown grass reminded me of the following verses:

"All flesh is like grass and all its glory like the flower of grass. The grass withers, and the flower falls, but the word of the Lord remains forever" (1 Peter 1:24–25).

"All flesh is grass, and all its beauty is like the flower of the field. The grass withers, the flower fades when the breath of the LORD blows on it; surely the people are grass. The grass withers, the flower fades, but the word of our God will stand forever" (Isaiah 40:6–8).

Yes, plants survive for a time, but then they die. The beauty of grass and flowers doesn't last, especially with a lack of water to feed and nourish the roots. How I love getting a small bouquet of flowers as a gift from my husband or as a treat for myself. They add such beauty and color to my kitchen and help me reflect on and bask in the beauty of God's creation. They give me joy. But they too only last for about one week, even with the powdered preservative put into the water after cutting the stems. But God's Word lasts for eternity. It is not short-lived. It will not vanish and die. God's Word regenerates us, as clearly seen in the verses above.

A common saying is: "Here today, gone tomorrow." People pass away, just like plants do. Material wealth or temporal items do the same. God's Word is permanent, and so is my salvation. It was given to me from Him for eternity. Colossians 3:2 states: "Set your minds on things that are above, not on things that are on earth." Earthly material possessions do not last. Hallelujah!

Listen to: "Glorious," by Paul Baloche.

My thoughts and prayer requests for today are:

WAITING EXPECTANTLY

Oh how I hate to wait for anything. While waiting in line at the grocery store, I keep telling myself, "I hope she hurries up." While waiting in a traffic jam, I am continually checking my speedometer, wanting it to move to a normal 70 mph to get to my destination. I remember how hard it was when I was a child to wait to open presents at Christmas. On Christmas Eve we got to open one present. On Christmas morning we would get to open the rest of the presents under the tree. It was so hard to get to sleep the night before!

Right now, waiting for those aphids on my greenhouse plants to die and be gone is hard to wait for, but I expect that it will eventually happen, thanks to the efforts of my various killing concoctions.

In Psalm 7:7, David wrote about waiting expectantly: "Be still before the LORD and wait patiently for him...." The HCSB words it this way: "Be silent before the LORD and wait expectantly for HIM...."

Stillness. Complete quietness. There is something very calming about seeing a sunrise or a sunset. It is quiet. There is no noise. This verse tells me that I must be still before the LORD when I bring my burdens and desires to Him. Then I must wait patiently and expectantly for Him. The NLT even says: "wait patiently for him to act." That's what is required. That is what I must do—wait expectantly.

At my church, we are expectantly waiting with excitement and expectation for the completion of our new building's renovations and the arrival of the move-in date! My husband is waiting on the Lord for the last of his double vision to go away completely. And I have a dream that I am waiting patiently for the Lord to bring about, if that is His will for me. But I have realized I am not always "still" or "silent" before my Lord as I wait—to just sit at His feet and tell Him, "Okay, I am here," as I look up into His face.

The word *wait* appears 106 times in the Bible. The book of Psalms uses it twenty-five times, and Isaiah mentions it eleven times. While we are in "the wait" for something, we often have expectations for what God will do. The King James Version actually says: "Rest in the LORD and wait patiently for him." Be still before the LORD. Be silent before the LORD. Rest in the LORD. Now, wait patiently and expectantly for Him. "Delight yourself in the LORD; and he will give you the desires of your heart. Commit your way to the LORD; trust in him, and he will act" (Psalm 37:4).

But there is one more event that I patiently and expectantly wait for: Christ's coming back for those who are His children. As 1 Corinthians 15:52 declares: "In a moment, in the twinkling of an eye, at the last trumpet. For the trumpet will sound, and the dead will be raised imperishable, and we shall be changed." Jesus told us in Revelation 22:7: "And behold, I am coming soon. Blessed is the one who keeps the words of the prophecy of this book." That phrase, "coming soon," keeps me waiting expectantly for Christ's return. A wall plaque that I received as a child says: "Perhaps today." I have it on my garage wall, right beside the door that enters our house, and it reminds me I am in the wait, and that I wait expectantly for my Savior's return. Hallelujah!

Listen to: "While I'm Waiting," by John Waller.

My thoughts and prayer requests for today are:

SELF-CONTROL

I have come to the realization that I am now in the age group of "the older women." I am a parent. I am a grandmother. I am eligible for the seniors' discount at the Soup Plantation restaurant. And July 27, 2015, marked my husband's and my forty-first wedding anniversary. I have been in my sales position in chemical and fine ingredients distribution for twenty-three years.

But as I continue in life, I realize more and more how hard self-control is—even as an older woman. My favorite cake is red velvet cake. I love red velvet cake, and I also love pizza. Our daughter, Amy, has kept up our family's tradition of making homemade pizza on the weekends. She has perfected working with Trader Joe's pizza dough, which requires just the right technique. We put on very healthy and low-fat toppings, but I have to have seconds and thirds, because, of course, she makes at least two or three different kinds. And of course, the pizza has a thin crust, so there are less calories, right? Unfortunately, I don't always abide by portion control, and then I pay for it later.

Titus 2:3–5 gives instructions to "older women": "Older women likewise are to be reverent in behavior, not slanderers or slaves to much wine. They are to teach what is good, and so train the young women to love their husbands and children, to be self-controlled, pure...."

Spiritual mothering is one of the greatest ministries God has given to the older women. We are to be examples to the younger women in our mentoring. We should be examples of living a self-controlled life in the faith. What does that look like? How I fall short in being a self-controlled mentor by example. I need to improve on controlling my food portions and, at times, my conversation. I tend to be very dogmatic about certain convictions, which is not necessarily bad. But using self-control for what comes out of my mouth would keep me from having turmoil and thoughts of self-condemnation after the fact.

As an older woman I must be an example in loving others. Paul wrote this passage as a mentor to a young man named Titus. He said that the older women were to teach the younger women how to love their husbands and their children. Praying for our mates, children, and friends is one important way that we reach out and love them. When we are continually in prayer for them, we will find it more difficult to boil over and give in to frustration. Once again, self-control comes into play. I often stoop beside our bed and touch my husband's pillow when I am praying fervently for him regarding some special need that he has. I have a picture on the windowsill in my office of our son, Jonathan, and his wife, Kim, which I look at when I pray for them. I also have a picture of our daughter, Amy, and her husband, David, next to Jonathan and Kim's picture, which reminds me to pray for them often as well. Praying for family is part of loving them and giving them grace.

Synonyms for self-control are: self-restraint, self-discipline, willpower, composure, moderation, and temperance. Overcoming self-indulgence is one definition for self-control. The fruits of the spirit all deal with self-control: love, joy, peace, patience, kindness, and goodness.

So I must be an example of self-control as I teach what is good to younger women. But what does that mean? How do I do that?

I must be an example of self-control by:
- Not giving into gossip.
- Not being addicted to food and wine. Not allowing any liberty to master me.
- Having good time management in my life.
- Honoring my husband and speaking highly of him.
- Keeping a humble spirit and guarding my heart against pride.
- Maintaining purity in my life.
- Showing unconditional love to my children.
- Desiring to love God and know Him more than anything else in my life.
- Having self-discipline in all matters by using moderation and temperance and not giving into gluttony or self-indulgence.

This is a sobering responsibility. It means teaching younger women—single or married—how to live in purity with moral excellence, while living in a sinful world; how to reflect Christ before others with integrity and as a testimony in their daily walk at work and in the home; and how to make a house a home—there is a difference. Then love, joy, peace, patience, kindness, and goodness will be a part of that home.

> Guide older women into lives of reverence so they end up as neither gossips nor drunks, but models of goodness. By looking at them, the younger women will know how to love their husbands and children, be virtuous and pure, keep a good house, be good wives. We don't want anyone looking down on God's Message because of their behavior" (Titus 2:3–5, MSG).

I have a lot of work to do to develop better self-control so that I can be a wiser mentor to younger women. As my pastor recently said in his sermon: "Wisdom is: I'll never do that again!" Much food for thought!

Listen to: "Beautiful Like This," by Josh Wilson.

My thoughts and prayer requests for today are:

WHEN I GROW UP

Do you remember wondering what you wanted to be when you grew up? I thought I wanted to be an elementary teacher. Everyone in my family at that time was either a teacher or a farmer, so my choice was to be a school teacher. That was not the career that I ended up in. I still wonder at times if I will *ever* grow up. When will I become fully mature in Christ and act like it?

Second Peter 1:3 (HCSB) states: "His divine power has granted to us everything required for life and godliness through the knowledge of Him who called us by His own glory and goodness." God has given me everything I need (through His Word) in order to live successfully. But why do I so often feel inadequate and insufficient? My self-doubt and insecurity pop up, even in my mature years. Insecurity doesn't disappear after those awkward teenage years.

In 2 Peter 1:3–10 Peter gives a list of seven qualities needed in order to keep from being useless or unfruitful in the knowledge of Jesus Christ. These qualities will keep us from being ineffective or unfruitful. They need to be evident and increasing in every believer's life. How I so desire to be used by God. Here are the qualities that Peter lists in this passage:

- Virtue (moral excellence)
- Knowledge
- Self-control
- Steadfastness (endurance)
- Godliness
- Brotherly affection
- Love

Peter tells us in verse 10 that if we practice these seven characteristics of a godly life, we will never stumble or fall. We must actively and diligently work at each of these areas in our lives. Personally, I want to be fruitful and grow in my knowledge of God. I want to have more faith. I want to love others better. I want to have more self-control. I must keep on keeping on in perseverance and in endurance in the uncertain crises of life as they occur. I must behave in reverence and deep respect for God and actively pursue a spiritual relationship with Him. This comes from keeping a heavenly mind-set, no matter what is bombarding me in life. I need to act properly and not react inappropriately. God needs to be my focus and to be at the center of my thoughts.

The definitions of the seven characteristics of a godly life are:

Developing virtue: That quality of life that makes someone stand out in excellence; having good character. It is our diligent devotion to personal righteousness.

Knowledge: Faith helps us to develop virtue, and virtue helps us to develop knowledge. This means understanding the truth of God's Word and applying it correctly. It means getting the precise and correct knowledge out of the passages we read. Gathering divine wisdom in an intimate and personal way to enable a stronger and more complete understanding of spiritual things is the goal. This involves diligently studying God's Word and not just relying on someone else's opinion.

Self-control: Some translations use the word *temperance*. When we control our anger, we are more mature in Christ. But controlling one's anger is not the only aspect in life wherein self-control is needed. In Peter's day, athletes were known to be self-restrained and to possess self-discipline. When there is moral excellence, guided by knowledge, discipline comes into play. Nothing should control us: such as food, drink, emotions, or even overspending. Moderation is the key.

Steadfastness and endurance: Patience is key, but it comes with practice. It is the ability to endure when circumstances are difficult. Self-control has to do with handling the pleasures of life, while steadfastness relates to handling the pressures and problems of life. John MacArthur said that perseverance is the spiritual staying power that will die before it gives in.

Godliness: "God-likeness" is a simple definition for this quality. It means living above the petty things in life—seeking to do the will of God in everything.

Brotherly affection: If we love Jesus Christ, we must love others. First John 5:1–2 states the fact that loving our sisters and brothers in Christ is the evidence that we are born of God.

Love: Our Lord was the prime example of showing love when He went to the cross. We must love in spite of the differences we have with our fellow believers.

Second Peter 1:3–10 is the message I want preached at my memorial service, when that day comes. It says it all. Developing and growing in these seven qualities will bring spiritual maturity and success in portraying the image of Christ.

> "For if these qualities are yours and are increasing, they keep you from being ineffective or unfruitful in the knowledge of our Lord Jesus Christ. For whoever

lacks these qualities is so nearsighted that he is blind" (2 Peter 1:8–9).

Don't we all go two steps forward and then one step backward in handling the "stuff" of life? When will I ever grow up?

Listen to: "Fix My Eyes on You," by for KING & COUNTRY.

My thoughts and prayer requests for today are:

ENSLAVED BY UNCERTAINTY

Do you ever feel tormented by feelings of uncertainty while going through a crisis—any crisis will do, not just the big ones? What about the last crisis you went through? Or what about a current crisis you are experiencing right now? I want closure. I want things fixed and to work right if they are faulty. "Things" are *supposed* to work right. When my husband gives instructions about doing something that needs to be done in the construction work he does, he expects the work to be done right. He expects his instructions to be followed so that he won't have to go back and fix them and do them over. But what about the things in life that go wrong and are out of our control?

I am currently going through a crisis with my cell phone not working properly due to the carrier my company has its corporate account with. I am not able to call the direct lines of the people within my office. Sometimes the calls go through; other times, they are not being connected. I recently had the same problem in my car as well. But I am bound to the cell phone carrier that the corporate account is under. The problem has been going on for four days, and the carrier's support team and I are becoming quite chummy, since we have now had more than four hours on the phone together. I was promised a callback within twenty-four hours. It hasn't happened.

Yesterday my patience and endurance in this crisis came to a screeching halt. It was hampering my sales job. I'd had it—along with pretty much everything else that I had put in a "problem" category surrounding my family and me this week. I felt like I was in the fairy tale of *The Princess and the Pea* by Hans Christian Andersen. Then I read the following verse in 2 Peter 2:9: "The Lord knows how to rescue the godly from trials."

I kept staring at that verse. Then I saw 1 Corinthians 10:13 (NIV): "No temptation has seized you except what is common to man. And God is faithful; He will not let you be tempted beyond what you can bear. But when you are tempted, He will also provide a way out so that you can stand up under it."

I started to pray for the cell carrier's technicians to be able to discover the solution to my irritating problem. Then I remembered that I had prayed earlier in the year that my boss would change his mind and let me go with a particular phone service provider. God can rescue me from this crisis. He can provide the solution. This is a common problem that God can get fixed. Nothing is too hard or too big that He cannot handle. Again, I must stop being enslaved by the uncertainty in this crazy crisis. I must again focus on God and trust Him for the way out. If it had not gone on this long, my problem might not have been recognized.

What are you going through right now? Are you in a calm state currently, or are you experiencing an anxious crisis yourself—be it big or small? In my book, *Taming the Lion's Roar: Handling Fear in the Midst of a Trial*, I wrote the following words in Lesson 3: "Fear Can Keep Us from Opportunities and Enslave Us in Uncertainty:

> "Focusing on the predicament may paralyze you, because the situation may seem humanly impossible. Focus instead on God and trust Him for the way out. That is all He needs to begin His work in you."

Time keeps ticking during an unresolved problem. It's the ticking clock that makes our frustration/anger fester. Time is the enemy—just like a bad hair day. Do you ever notice that you talk faster when you are trying to find a quick resolution?

Eleanor Roosevelt is quoted as saying: "You gain strength, courage, and confidence by every experience in which you really stop to look fear in the face. You are able to say to yourself, 'I've lived through the horror. I can take the next thing that comes along.'"

God has answered prayers in the past. He will answer my cell phone nightmare. Satan's weapons against us are guilt, shame, frustration, and failure. I am sighing right now from weariness in not being able to move beyond my problem that has not yet had closure, and I am feeling like a failure for not maintaining the right attitude. I will stand up, stand firm, and keep praying for the end of my irritating crisis, because it will end eventually. I will persevere and have complete faith that God will change this situation somehow—and this too shall pass. How about you? Are you being stretched in not getting relief from a current crisis—be it big or small? God will show you mercy. When God imparts His grace and mercy it is like healing of a cut or wound that was red, swollen, and painful. When the pain is gone, it is so good! Cling to Him and don't let any crisis enslave you. Focusing on the predicament will enslave you. Instead, focus on heavenly things, because Christ is sitting at the right hand of God. A better day is coming!

> "The steadfast love of the LORD never ceases; his mercies never come to an end; they are new every morning; great is your faithfulness." Lamentations 3:23-24

Listen to: "Thrive," by Casting Crowns.,

My thoughts and prayer requests for today are:

HARVEST TIME

I was born in rural Northwest Iowa. Farming is very big there. I can remember that every August, a church in my hometown would set aside a whole evening to pray for the crops and the farmers in that community. Rainy and sunny days were both important. Springtime weather was critical in getting the crop planted and in the ground. Proper numbers of days of sunshine and warm weather after the snow thawed were important to the growth of corn and soybeans. By July 4, the corn was supposed to be knee-high. An early frost and snow in the fall could be devastating. The Thanksgiving holiday was centered on giving thanks that the corn was picked and harvested. The total yield was always important. Now people post on Facebook that the beans are in or the corn is in, signifying that the harvest is done.

The same is true for crops in Southern California. Usually in October, the growers have a harvest party, celebrating the fact that all the grapes are picked, crushed, processed, and bottled. There is an abundant amount of food prepared and brought out. It is equally hard work, and a time of celebration is due when the grape harvest is done. Weather is equally important for the outcome of the crops here. Did they have enough hot weather? Was it too hot too long? They need the temperatures to be between 81 and 94 degrees. Did they have too many cloudy days? Too many days near the 100-degree mark can be devastating. Each vintage year is different, due to the weather affecting the growing season of their crops.

> "You have put more joy in my heart than they have when their grain and wine abound" (Psalm 4:7).

> "They rejoice before you as with joy at the harvest, as they are glad when they divide the spoil" (Isaiah 9:3).

The outcomes of our lives are not dependent on the weather. Sunshine, heat, fog, rain, or cool temperatures do not determine our worth. Yes, there is much rejoicing when the harvesting of crops is completed, but God gives us more joy than any abundance of harvests that any farm group will ever have. When any prayer request of mine is answered, my heart zings for joy!

Luke 15:7 declares: "There will be more joy in heaven over one sinner who repents than over ninety-nine righteous persons who need no repentance." When a person accepts Jesus Christ as his or her Lord and Savior and gives testimony to it, that individual's face glows with a pure joy that only God can give.

Peter also talked about joy in 1 Peter 1:8: "Though you do not now see him, you believe in him and rejoice with joy that is inexpressible and filled with glory." Yes, that is the right description of more joy than at any harvest: "inexpressible."

Psalm 28:7 (NIV) reiterates this: "The LORD is my strength and my shield; my heart trusts in him and he helps me. My heart leaps for joy, and with my song I praise him."

God's personal blessings are greater than the yield of any crop that can be planted and harvested. The KJV says it this way in Psalm 4:7: "Thou has put gladness in my heart, more than when their corn and their wine increased." Any material joy cannot compare with the spiritual joy that comes from our Lord.

There is abundant joy from His presence. We oftentimes describe it just as Scripture does: as a joy that is unspeakable and full of glory.

I am trying to develop a new habit every morning during my God-and-I time: giving thanks back to God. I am writing down three to four things that I am thankful for each morning. This brings my mind back to praising God for the pure joy He has given me in my life. This morning I wrote down four things in my prayer journal that I am thankful for: (1) Getting to live very close to our grandchildren and children. (2) My husband's faithful habit of having us pray together every night before we go to sleep. (3) A friend who keeps encouraging me to write more. (4) My husband's double vision is going away, and his ophthalmologist saw improvement at his checkup yesterday. And there is so much more that I could write and share with you that I am currently thankful for! God daily shows me His divine grace and mercy! My prayer is that you will have an increasing joy in your heart as you reflect on and recall the things for which you feel gratitude and for which you have a heart of thanksgiving.

We need to have more than one holiday a year on which we set aside time to give God thanks for the things He has provided. This will put a joy in our hearts that will be greater than any abundant grain and wine harvest around!

Listen to: "Listen to our Hearts," by Casting Crowns.

My thoughts and prayer requests for today are:

THE HELPER

As I continue to mature in life, I have noticed that my memory is not as sharp as it used to be. For example, when I bought groceries this morning, how did I forget to buy blueberries? My husband has them on his oatmeal every morning for breakfast, and he used the last of them up today. I am also bad at remembering people's names. Faces I remember, and as far as what someone was wearing, I have no problem. But their name often escapes me. Thank goodness for Facebook so I can look people up when I have that option!

When Jesus was meeting with the disciples before the Feast of the Passover—when He knew His hour had come, He started by washing the disciples' feet. Then He asked them if they understood what He had done for them. He was being an example to them. Next He foretold of one who would betray Him. Then He gave them a new commandment: to love one another, as it says in John 13:35: "By this all people will know that you are my disciples, if you have love for one another."

Jesus next told His disciples that He was going to prepare a place for them, and if they knew Him, they knew God. But in John 14, we read that Thomas said to him, "Lord, we do not know where you are going. How can we know the way?" Jesus simply replied: "I am the way, and the truth, and the life. No one comes to the Father except through me. If you had known me, you would have known my Father also. From now on you do know him and have seen him" (John 14:6–7). Jesus follows that conversation with words of assurance that: "If you ask anything in my name, this I will do, that the Father may be glorified in the Son. If you ask me anything in my name, I will do it" (John 14:14). That is why when I end every prayer, I say, "In Jesus's name, Amen."

Jesus was leading up to telling His disciples of His coming departure to heaven to be with His Father. He then tells his disciples that God will be sending a helper, called the Holy Spirit.

John 14:26 states:

> "But the Helper, the Holy Spirit, whom the Father will send in my name, he will teach you all things and bring to your remembrance all that I have said to you."

The Holy Spirit would remind his disciples what Jesus had taught them and would teach them all things. The Holy Spirit would bring to their memory all that Jesus had said to them.

The Holy Spirit will teach me as well and bring to my memory all that Jesus has said to me so that I can depend on God's Word in difficult times. I need to memorize God's Word more, because when things come up in life, a verse will come to memory to help me combat worry, doubts, and basically a lack of faith on my part. I will know God by knowing His Word. By keeping a mind-set of heavenly mind control, Scripture will come into my thoughts and push out Satan's weapons of temptations in my mind as the Holy Spirit brings verses of light from the Word of God.

My memory may be short regarding day-to-day tasks or people's names. But I want my mind to be quick at remembering God's Word. I want to be remembered as a mature and godly woman in Christ.

Proverbs 10:7 states: "The memory of the righteous is a blessing, but the name of the wicked will rot."

We have various apps to remind us of things to do. We have a calendar on our smartphones so that we can set an alarm to remind us to be somewhere and to tell us what time to be there. There are various word and picture association aids that can help us remember people's names. But even better, we have the Holy Spirit to convict our conscience, to teach us all things, and to bring to our memory all that God has said in His Word. The Spirit uses His Word to give us His peace, His love, His joy, and His comfort. The Holy Spirit, the Helper, will bring to our memory all that God has said to us through His Word.

Listen to: "To Know You," by Casting Crowns.

My thoughts and prayer requests for today are:

TOMORROW

Yesterday was my husband's and my forty-first wedding anniversary. The day was beautiful and sunny—not too hot, since it was July 27th. We greatly anticipated our wedding anniversary celebration dinner. We went to a special restaurant that we had never been to before, but it was closed. After all, it was a Monday, and many restaurants are not open on Mondays.

So then we went to a favorite, quiet Italian pizza place, and we were the only ones in the whole restaurant that night. We reminisced and reflected in general on how we had come through so many hard times in life together, and we wondered what the next set of years would bring. Later that evening, before going to bed, my husband noticed that the carpet was wet in the bedroom at the end of the hall. It was only wet next to the wall and in the closet. We hadn't anticipated this. He opened the door where the furnace and air conditioner condenser were and found the problem: the air conditioner drain was plugged and had backed up, causing water to accumulate underneath the carpet on the floor.

My husband went over to the neighbor's house, explained to him what was going on, and unclogged our air conditioner drain that ran over the wall and onto the neighbor's property. Then my husband spent hours using his Shop-Vac® to suck up all the water from under the carpet and air conditioner space. This took him at least two hours. It reminded me of the verse in Proverbs 27:1: "Do not boast about tomorrow, for you do not know what a day may bring forth."

Isn't that true? We had no idea that our evening would end up with him having to take care of a wet cement floor and trying to figure out if we had a mold and mildew problem to take care of as well. It took him a great deal of time to determine just what the extent of this air conditioner drain plug up would be and how much work it would involve. This was another instance in life that was out of our control. As my husband said that night, "Isn't there always something?"

Yes, each day brings about its own surprises. We don't know what tomorrow may bring. But God does. He knows what our today and our tomorrow will unfold. I remember singing an old song in my teenage years regarding not knowing about tomorrow. It said to just live from day to day. It went on to say: "Many things about tomorrow, I don't seem to understand. But I know who holds the future, and I know who holds my hand."

Remember Jeremiah 29:11: "For I know the plans I have for you, declares the LORD, plans to prosper you and not to harm you, plans to give you hope and a future."

My prayer for today: *God, You know what is ahead of me for today. You will walk each step with me and even ride in my car beside me as I drive to each sales appointment today. I need Your wisdom in what to say and when. May I be obedient to You and keep my thoughts on You. My life is in Your hands. Use me. Bless me. May I be of benefit to others. I don't want to embarrass You by anything I say or do, dear Lord. Don't let me say stupid stuff today. May I leave a good memory in the minds of people I come in contact with today, and may I glorify You in my integrity. In Jesus's name, Amen!*

Listen to: "I Refuse," by Josh Wilson.

My thoughts and prayer requests for today are:

I HAVE EVERYTHING I NEED

Recently a customer of mine said to me that he and his wife would be celebrating their forty-third wedding anniversary, and he boldly stated that he had everything he ever wanted in life. He is not, as he told me, a born-again Christian. This caused me to consider and give thought to my own life: Could I say the same? As I further reflect and grasp the importance of keeping my mind focused on things above, where Christ sits at the right hand of God (Colossians 3:1), and having a heavenly mind-set (Colossians 3:2), I am at the place where I need to pause. I have pushed the proverbial icon on my life to "pause" in order to examine myself before I can say I truly have everything I have ever wanted in life.

But as a believer in Christ, it is not about "me." It is about bringing glory to my heavenly Father, who is preparing a mansion for me in eternity. As the song says, "This world is not my home. I'm just a passin' through." My treasures are not of this world. There is a practical application of this in Colossians 3:5, 10: "Put to death therefore what is earthly in you: sexual immorality, impurity, passion, evil desire, and covetousness, which is idolatry. Put on the new self, which is being renewed in knowledge after the image of its creator."

We are to take off the old self and put on the new self, being formed into the image of Christ. It is like taking off old clothes and putting on new clothes. I want my life to reflect the image of Christ and not the old or former me. I need to push a heavenly mind-set rebooting key when I find myself tempted to be jealous of some other woman's house, vacations, or clothes. It is just stuff. This really is my own self-centeredness, and it signifies that I am not being content with what God has given me. I need to shred those selfish thoughts and put on righteousness, grasp more knowledge from God's Word, and put it into practice. Then I will truly have everything I have ever wanted.

In Philippians 4:8, God tells me what my mind-set is supposed to be: "Finally, brothers, whatever is true, whatever is honorable, whatever is just, whatever is pure, whatever is lovely, whatever is commendable, if there is any excellence, if there is anything worthy of praise, think about these things."

Developing a heavenly mind-set and focusing on having a heavenly mind control is just that: reflecting on past answers to prayers, thanking God for what He has graciously given us, and meditating on precious verses that He has spoken to us through.

I too can say, as Paul said in Philippians 4:11, "Not that I am speaking of being in need, for I have learned in whatever situation I am to be content. I know how to be brought low, and I know how to abound. In any and every circumstance, I have learned the secret of facing plenty and hunger, abundance and need."

Can I say that I have everything I have ever wanted? No. But I can say that I have everything I will ever need because of God's gracious provisions for my life. I can say that I am content. My responsibility is to keep my thoughts centered on Christ, who is seated at the right hand of God, where I will spend eternity with Him. How about you?

> "If then you have been raised with Christ, seek the things that are above, where Christ is, seated at the right hand of God. Set your minds on things that are above, not on things that are on earth. For you have died, and your life is hidden with Christ in God.

When Christ who is your life appears, then you also will appear with him in glory" (Colossians 3:1–4).

Listen to: "Lord, I Need You," by Chris Tomlin, and also to: "My Worth Is Not in What I Own" by Keith and Kristyn Getty.

My thoughts and prayer requests for today are:

_____

_____

_____

_____

_____

_____

_____

_____

_____

_____

_____

_____

_____

_____

_____

_____

_____

ABOUT THE AUTHOR

Linda Killian lives in California. She and her husband have been married for forty-one years and have two grown children, Jonathan Killian and Amy Studarus, and three grandchildren: Tate and Harper Studarus and Brynley Killian. Linda works full time as an outside sales representative for a raw materials and fine ingredients manufacturer and distributor. She is coordinator for her church's Women of the Word ministry and has served on the Women of the Word Bible study teaching team. Linda has one published Bible study book available: *Taming the Lion's Roar: Handling Fear in the Midst of a Trial*. Linda has a passion for moving women to positions of strength found in God's Word.

***

This particular book actually came out of a request from my mother. She wanted something new to read as a devotional every morning. She enjoyed my Bible study book on handling fear and continues to go through it. She has read the Bible through for several years, but now she wanted something new to help focus her mind on God first thing in the morning. She wanted something a bit more condensed that would draw her mind heavenward. I had taught two sections from Colossians at my church. One lesson was centered on having a heavenly mind control. The more I studied and prepared, the more I realized the importance of keeping my mind on heavenly things rather than earthly things. It was a life-changing experience that involved rebooting my mind toward disciplining my thoughts—and even my daydreams—on things above, rather than on things of this earth. I realized that this was to be a priority—on a daily basis. This was the devotional book that my mother and I both needed—and that I trust other women need as well. This book is based on my true-life experiences. I have felt these emotions, crying and laughing just like you.

Made in the USA
San Bernardino, CA
31 January 2016